Krish Kandiah is Executive Director for Churches in Mission at the Evangelical Alliance and Theological Advisor to Tearfund. Krish has been a missionary in Albania, a pastor in Harrow, and a faculty member at Oxford University. He is a husband, father and foster carer. He is in demand as a Bible teacher and runs an award-winning blog at http://krishk.com

Krish Kandiah's other books:

Yahweh: God in all his fullness (Authentic Media, 2006)

Destiny: What's life all about? (Monarch, 2007)

Twenty-Four: Integrating faith and real life (Authentic Media, 2007)

FRESH: Bite-sized inspirations for new students (IVP, 2008)

Life Swap: Finding the life you always wanted (Monarch, 2008)

One Hope: A personal journal (Authentic Media, 2008)

How to Save a Life (Authentic Media, 2009)

Dysciples: Why I fall asleep when I pray and twelve other discipleship dysfunctions (Authentic Media, 2009)

Square Mile: Four weeks of Bible study for personal use (Authentic Media, 2009)

FINAL: Bite-sized inspirations for final-year students (IVP, 2010)

Just Politics (Authentic Media, 2010)

Route 66: A crash course in navigating life with the Bible (Monarch, 2011)

Home for Good (Hodder, 2013)

BACK TO THE SOURCE

 **CHALLENGES TO BE, SAY,
AND DO LIFE THE JESUS WAY**
(WHEN YOU ARE NOT THE SON OF GOD
AND SAVIOUR OF THE WORLD)

KRISH KANDIAH

MONARCH
BOOKS

Oxford, UK and Grand Rapids, Michigan, USA

Published by Monarch Books (an imprint of Lion Hudson plc)
Wilkinson House, Jordan Hill Road, Oxford OX2 8DR, England
Email: monarch@lionhudson.com www.lionhudson.com / monarch
and by Elevation (an imprint of the Memralife Group)
Memralife Group, 14 Horsted Square, Uckfield, East Sussex TN22 1QG
Tel: +44 (0)1825 746530; Fax: +44 (0)1825 748899;
www.elevationmusic.com

ISBN 978 0 85721 441 6
e-ISBN 978 0 85721 440 9

First edition 2013

With thanks to Hodder Faith who released the author   H
from a previous commitment in order to write this book. HODDER &
                                                         STOUGHTON

Acknowledgments

All other scripture quotations taken from the Holy Bible, Today's New International
Version. Copyright © 2004 by International Bible Society. Used by permission of
Hodder & Stoughton Publishers. A member of the Hachette Livre UK Group. All
rights reserved. 'TNIV' is a registered trademark of International Bible Society.
Scripture taken from *The Message*. Copyright © by Eugene H. Peterson 1993, 1994,
1995, 1996, 2000, 2001, 2002. Used by permission of NavPress Publishing Group.

A catalogue record for this book is available from the British Library

Printed and bound in the UK, February 2013, LH27

CONTENTS

Do It Like Jesus

INTRODUCTION

"Of course I want to be more like Jesus. Who wouldn't? He is the wisest, kindest, strongest person ever to have graced this planet. He changed people's lives. He changed history. I'd love to be like that. But then again, I'm not sure I could cope with living quite as publicly as he did. I don't really 'do' people very well, and especially where there is conflict or controversy involved. Also, I draw the line at facing torture and execution.

"Of course I want to say wise and wonderful words like Jesus did, but it's an impossible ask. I never know the right thing to say, and often I say completely the wrong thing. Whenever I open my mouth I have the knack of putting my foot in it. My jokes and stories fall a little flat, and whenever I talk about God and my faith, I seem to trip over my words. Nobody will ever listen to me like they listened to Jesus.

"Of course I want to do what Jesus did, but it's a tough job. He lived such a good life that even his enemies couldn't fault him. Whereas, if you ask any of my friends, they could happily reel off a whole list of my shortcomings. People tend to get more ill after I intercede for them, whereas Jesus healed all sorts of people. Jesus literally shone with the glory of God, while I prefer to keep my faith under cover.

"I know that Jesus is the eternal God who existed before the universe began. He lives in a faultless relationship with God the Father and God the Holy Spirit since eternity past and for an endless future. Jesus is the perfect and incomparable Almighty God, the only one who could pay for the sins of the world. His life is unrivalled by any other person that has ever walked the earth. His thirty years on earth have influenced everything about life as we know it. I know that Jesus is unique. Therefore being like Jesus in everything he was, said and did is, surely, impossible.

"But I crave to be perfect as he was perfect. I long to make a difference and see the world transformed around me. I wish I knew what to say and how to say it in every encounter of my day.

"Of course I want to be like Jesus, but I am not the Son of God and Saviour of the World, and I never can be.

"Can I really live out Jesus' extraordinary lifestyle in my ordinary circumstances?

"Can I really be like Jesus, do what Jesus did, speak as Jesus spoke?"

To find out we need to go *Back to the Source*. Jesus is the source of our eternal life, because of all that he did for us through his life, death and resurrection. But he is also the source for our life now. Through his Spirit he empowers us to live like him in his world, to make difficult decisions, develop new habits and become a new counter-cultural community of believers. The Spirit opens up the source code of the Christian faith; through the Scriptures he reboots our imaginations, refreshes our vision of Christ, reinvigorates our heart for God and reshapes our dreams and aspirations. As we go *Back to the Source* we will find new confidence, new life and new power to BE, SAY and DO like Jesus.

We want to BE, SAY and DO like Jesus, because this is the way he made us. Like a piano awaits a maestro to play it. Like clay awaits a potter. Like canvas awaits a painter. Like a wilderness awaits a gardener. Like a problem awaits a solution. Our lives long to be shaped by Jesus.

Living like Jesus does not mean you will have no use for bridges or swimming gear because you will have learned to walk on water. Living like Jesus will not render lifts and escalators unnecessary because you have learned the skill of ascension. There is no secret formula hidden in this book that will clone you into a modern-day messiah. You can never be the Son of God and Saviour of the World.

But because God made you to be like Jesus, calls you to follow him and sends his Spirit to make you more like him, there is hope. There are habits and attitudes and passions and inspirations and meditations and disciplines and role models and visual aids and real-life examples that are offered in Scripture and explored in this book. As you discover these out of a desire to live like Jesus, you may find that your lives connect with Jesus in many more ways than the thirty suggested in these chapters.

How to read this book

This book is best read slowly. Every time I start up my computer it asks for a password. I could type that nine-letter password in the dark, without looking at the keyboard, in less than a second. But ask me to draw a map of the keyboard I type on, and I couldn't do it. I have developed a form of "muscle memory".[1] Through practice and repetition I have developed an automatic response whenever I open my laptop. In the Christian life it is possible to develop patterns of behaviour that help us to be good, think good and do good almost instinctively.[2] This book aims to drip feed some ideas about how to start on this journey. By reading them one chapter a day, you will allow your brain time to reflect on and acclimatize to each idea before moving on to the next one. Simply reading each chapter would be about as useful as reading a book about typing without actually practising at a keyboard, so questions for further thought are included. These questions are designed to bring about life transformation. Alternatively, find your own way of reflecting on, discussing and taking action on each idea, so that Christ's character shapes your whole life, and you react and respond to everything in life in a Christlike way.

This book is best read in company. God makes us Christlike in three main ways: through his Holy Spirit, through his holy word and through his holy people. All of these intersect: God's Spirit unites us to other believers and helps us to understand Scripture; God's word instructs us to be part of a church family; and it is through being a part of a family of believers that God equips and encourages us to keep going in the pursuit of Christlike character. This book will be useful to you if you read it on your own. But you will find it even more helpful if you are able to read it with other people, either through a reading group, a cell group or, better still, the whole church reading it together.

Three ways to use this book

1. A six-week course looking at five chapters a week. Readers could aim to digest one chapter a day from Monday to Friday. This could be paralleled with six sermons, two each on the topics BE, SAY and DO like Jesus.

2. A one-month course looking at one chapter a day. Readers could aim to digest one chapter a day for a month. This could be paralleled with four sermons, one each on BE, SAY and DO like Jesus, and either an introductory sermon or a concluding sermon or both.

3. A three-week course, looking at ten chapters a week. Readers could aim to digest two chapters a day for a month. This could be paralleled with three sermons, one each on BE, SAY and DO like Jesus.

The stories in each chapter (some are true, others are fictional) serve not only to ground the chapter, but also to provoke discussion. The questions and challenges for further thought are designed to guide quiet times or home groups.

BE IT LIKE JESUS

CHAPTER 1

BE ICONIC

Monday, 6.10 a.m.

Pearl has been awake a while. Time of the day makes little difference to her. Her radio is her main form of company and she's glad it's a twenty-four-hour service nowadays.

This morning she listens to an audio recording of the Sunday service from the church she used to attend faithfully but now seldom visits. She listens regularly to the recordings and sometimes she even sings along with the hymns.

The preacher this particular morning is passionate about the fact that we serve a missionary God. He challenges and commissions his congregation to go out in God's power to the four corners of the world.

A tear forms in Pearl's eye. She can only just manage to reach the four corners of her sheltered accommodation. Every week Christianity feels more and more like a whole list of things she will never manage to do. She pauses the sermon and feels more alone and incapacitated than ever.

I remember the day when I decided to kill an elderly grandmother. It wasn't an easy decision. It was either her or a sickly teenager. One of them had to go. I was in school at the time, and each class member had to vote on whom to throw out of a hypothetical hot-air balloon that was losing altitude, risking the lives of the five people on board. The only ballast left to jettison was the doctor, the aid worker, the President of the USA, the teenager on kidney dialysis or the 94-year-old grandmother. The class voted unanimously to sacrifice the grandmother.

In this famous moral dilemma known as "the balloon debate",[1] the intention of my teacher was to educate my class in the skills of ethical argument. But there was a distinct sub-message being communicated: that people are to be valued by what they do rather than by who they are. Sometimes it seems the church and the culture we live in may be in cahoots concerning this tendency to value "human doings" more than human beings. If the church had a balloon debate, it would probably send Pearl hurtling towards the earth without a parachute while the pastor and worship leader and Sunday School teacher looked on from the gondola.

A key principle in understanding the Christian faith is that our value as humans is dependent not on what we do, or how useful we are to others or to society, but on who we are. But working out how to BE human is not as easy as it sounds. It is much easier to shift the focus onto what we DO or what we SAY. Although those things are important too, they have to be understood in the context of our fundamental identity.

Right at the beginning of the Bible, in the chapters that describe the origins of humanity, we are given a not-so-subtle clue as to what that fundamental identity is all about:

Then God said, "Let us make human beings in our image, in our likeness, so that they may rule over the fish in the sea and the birds in the sky, over the livestock and all the wild animals, and over all the creatures that move along the ground."

So God created human beings in his own image, in the image of God he created them; male and female he created them.[2]

Three times in this passage we are reminded that our primary identity is as image-bearers of God. The Greek word for "image" is *eikon* from which we get our word "icon". An icon on a computer desktop symbolically represents a function of a computer program; for example, if you see the image of a trash can or an envelope, it helps you to know what to press to delete a file or to email someone. Similarly, we, as icons, represent God, his character and his purposes in the world, and help others to access him.

This iconic status is absolute: it is not something we can choose or something we can lose. Every human being, regardless of age, ability, gender, race, income level, personal hygiene, sexual orientation or faith, is made in the image of God. To BE ICONIC means to be "visible bodies that reflect the glory of God",[3] as God created us.

Because human beings were created by God as icons of his character, every person is intrinsically and equally valuable. Our value is based on this privilege, not on how well we think we, or others, measure up to this description.

God makes this very clear in the creation account, and also reiterates it a couple of chapters later, after the tragic description of how sin had entered the world and marred God's perfect creation with rebellion, resentment and murder.[4] In case we are in any doubt, even as fallen and sinful human beings, we are still made in God's image.

In order to understand what this means in practice, we must look to Jesus. He is described as being *the* image-bearer of the invisible God.[5] He is our role model and example in understanding our own identity.

First of all, being image-bearers alongside Jesus has powerful implications for how we see ourselves. Jesus was keenly aware that everything about him demonstrated the character of God. When people saw and knew Jesus, they saw and knew the Father. Jesus had such a clear sense of identity that he was not swayed by public opinion or seduced by popularity or swamped by self-doubt. Whether he was attracting crowds and gaining followers, or being abandoned and betrayed, he never lost that sense of reflecting his Father's glory and character and will.

Secondly, we see that Jesus demonstrates that everyone else is to be valued independently of what they have done or can do. Jesus made time for people whom others would have normally ignored: those with disabilities and illnesses, children, women, the poor, the outsiders. He offered them love, honour and respect. He treated them with value, grace and dignity. Even in his choice of friends and disciples, he did not behave like a premiership football manager collecting the most eloquent, efficient and energetic dream team. Jesus picked a bunch of ordinary people from all sorts of walks of life, and with all sorts of shortcomings. He called those who were left out and left behind. He listened to the cry of the destitute and took time to touch the untouchable.

The five people in my balloon debate were to be measured by who could contribute the most to a consumerist society. Those who fell short had one last chance to be useful by becoming disposable bags of ballast to be cast out for the benefit of the greater good.

Jesus, the Creator God and sustainer of the universe, ultimately demonstrated our intrinsic value as God's created people. When the time came to choose who would be sacrificed to save the lives of the rest of the world, Jesus jumped out of the figurative balloon himself, dying for us all.

Being iconic means we understand our fundamental identity as representatives of God. This identity involves how we see ourselves, how we relate to God and how we relate to other people. Being iconic means we understand that (in the words of A. F. Holmes) "to abuse a person, to violate her rights, is to disrespect God and depreciate his image in her. It is in effect an act of blasphemy, for the sanctity of persons reflects the sanctity of God."[6] Being iconic means treating every other person we come across with the same value, grace and dignity as God shows us, refusing to measure their worth by their economic or social contribution to society. Being iconic means becoming more secure that we, and others, are intrinsically and infinitely valuable.

Being iconic is not something we can earn or buy or achieve. It is an unchangeable status that we can appreciate and enjoy, and affirm in everything we are and do and say, ensuring that others around us know this truth too.

Pearl wipes the tear from her eye. She may not be much practical use to anyone these days, but she thanks God for loving her so much.

She doesn't know it, but one of the teenagers with whom she often chatted after church services has chosen Pearl as her role model in life. Lauren said, "I love Pearl. She really seems to care about me and is so positive about everything, even though she has a lot of pain and troubles in her own life."

Pearl's home help also knew there was something different about Pearl. Shirley said: "Many of the people I work with treat me like a resented personal slave. Pearl treated me like a real person. Nobody had ever offered to pray for me before, and as I asked her about her faith, I knew she was telling the truth. It shone out of her face. It was because of Pearl I became a Christian."

For further thought

BE: *reflection*. What difference should knowing that we are made in God's image make to the way we view ourselves?

SAY: *discussion*. What would you say to Pearl if she came to you feeling low because she felt too incapacitated to do anything for God?

How is everything we do and say affected by the way we view ourselves? Talk about some of the things you have done and said today and what they reveal about your identity.

DO: *action*. How will we treat others around us differently because of what we have reflected on today?

CHAPTER 2

BE GLORIOUS

Johnny was having a self-image crisis. A critical email had pinged into his inbox, and its tone and demands were so harsh he was struggling to get his mind down to any work. He was supposed to be editing photographs from the wedding shoot at the weekend, but as he removed blemishes from the bride's face and readjusted the waistline of the groom, the email was playing on his mind.

It would be nice if he could Photoshop his own life, not just his work, airbrushing out his own faults and failings. It would be even better if he could Photoshop his rude and unappreciative clients in the flesh. And if he got good at it, he could take on a harder challenge, the likes of Adolf Hitler, Osama Bin Laden or Norwegian mass-murderer Andreas Brevik. Johnny found it almost as hard to imagine them being made in God's image, as he found it hard to understand that he himself was made in God's image.

Images were Johnny's work, his passion. He knew there were good images and bad images. This morning, thanks to that email, he felt pretty low down on the scale.

Knowing we are made in the image of God is an incredible privilege that brings us freedom, joy, peace, hope, security and iconic status. Knowing that we are made in the image of God can also bring with it an incredible sense of failing. Whether we struggle to appreciate what we see in the mirror, or whether we battle to hold our tongue; whether we fail to treat others with dignity or fail to live by God's standards, we can feel that we constantly let God and ourselves down.

We all, as the Bible says, "fall short of the glory of God".[1] From Mother Teresa to Adolf Hitler and all the rest of us in between, we struggle on a daily basis to adequately live up to our status as made in the image of God.

This shortfall between our iconic status as God's image-bearers and our constant state of inability to live up to that in our day-to-day lives is a reminder of why we need Jesus. He is the one who represented God perfectly, as we should. Jesus is the one who treated everyone with value, as we should. Jesus, in every moment of his life and his death, showed the world around him what God our Father is like, just as we should.

But our daily failure to represent God as committed followers of Jesus should not drive us to despair. It is exactly because Jesus lived the perfect iconic life and died and was raised from the dead and lives in us today, that those feelings of inadequacy can drive us to BE GLORIOUS.

Paul writes to a struggling church:

Now the Lord is the Spirit, and where the Spirit of the Lord is, there is freedom. And we all, who with unveiled faces contemplate the Lord's glory, are being transformed into his image with ever-increasing glory, which comes from the Lord, who is the Spirit.[2]

There is a conundrum here. How can we be transformed into God's image, if we are already image-bearers? The Bible seems to teach about both *being* the image of God and *becoming* the image of God.

Imagine a couple twenty-four hours after their wedding ceremony. They have made vows, been declared man and wife by the presiding official, exchanged rings and enjoyed their wedding night together. They are 100 per cent married. There are no other legal requirements that need meeting. Yet, God willing, over the next year, ten years, fifty years, they will discover and experience so much more about their marriage, even though they will never be any more married than they were the day after the ceremony.[3]

This illustration helps us to understand the conundrum of being God's image-bearers. Although we are always 100 per cent iconic, we can grow into our identity, and discover and experience at a deeper level what this means. We are born in the image of God, and nothing can change that fact of our identity, but the sin in our lives means that we are actually a disfigured caricature of the character of God. When we become Christians, God fully accepts us as we are into his family and begins to transform us into the likeness of his perfect image-bearer, his Son Jesus Christ.

We have a lot to learn and experience and develop when it comes to representing God as Jesus did. These verses not only remind us of this, but they also motivate us with the promise of ever-increasing glory.

What is meant by "glory" here? Paul is referring to the incident where Moses sees a little of the glory of God from his hiding place in the cleft of the rock. The experience left him with a physically glowing face that he had to veil from the Israelites so they weren't afraid. But Moses heard more about the glory of God than he saw of it. As God passed by Moses he spoke the following words:

The Lord, the Lord, the compassionate and gracious God, slow to anger, abounding in love and faithfulness, maintaining love to thousands, and forgiving wickedness, rebellion and sin.[4]

Notice this list of character qualities. They are not dissimilar to the fruit of the Spirit that Paul lists in Galatians.[5] Being glorious primarily means reflecting these characteristics of God, which the Holy Spirit wants to develop in us over time.

Letting the Holy Spirit transform us into the likeness of Jesus is not achieved by an immediate makeover or a one-off experience in a church meeting. This transformation process is less like the instant filters on Photoshop and more like the painstaking work that an expert restorer will apply to a priceless painting by a grand master over the course of months, years or decades.

We are to be both iconic and glorious, just as Jesus was. We see these two descriptions of Jesus side by side in this verse by the writer to the Hebrews: "the radiance of God's glory and the exact representation of his being".[6]

As we seek to be like Jesus in our daily lives by both being and becoming image-bearers, we can be confident that the Holy Spirit is working to transform us more into God's image and God's glory. This process works itself out in the daily routines of our lives, in the emails we send, the affections we show, the thought-patterns we habituate,[7] the decisions we make and the people we meet. These are the seedbed of our transformation as we grow more like God in our character, and learn to BE GLORIOUS like Jesus.

Johnny looked at the image on his monitor. His own frown and frustrations contrasted with the relaxed smiles from the wedding shoot.

He knew that his work was an opportunity to help people value the vows they had made by capturing and celebrating the joy of their wedding. He prayed that this couple would know God's grace for their marriage. Just as these photos needed a lot of work to help them look their best, he asked for God's help in his own life so he could reflect God's best too.

He drafted an email response as calmly and graciously as he could, before returning to some final touch-ups.

For further thought

BE: *reflection*. When do you find it hardest to accept that you are made in God's image or that you are born to be glorious?

SAY: *discussion*. How have you already experienced the transformation that the Holy Spirit brings in your life to make you more like Jesus? How have you seen others transformed? Spend some time encouraging one another.

What advice would you give to a Christian who was caught in a pattern of sinful behaviour they can't seem to break out of?

DO: *action*. Which area is God transforming in your life at the moment? What can you do today to practise that?

CHAPTER 3

BE TRUE

Wednesday, 10.50 a.m.

As she walked into the management meeting Sal was consciously aware that she was the youngest person in the room. The other managers were all middle-aged men – and constantly going on about the football. She feigned interest – scanning the headlines before work so she could manage a few well-placed informed questions about the latest win or scandal. They were planning a golf day for a few weeks' time, but it was men only, so she tried not to look like it mattered to her. She felt excluded and wished she didn't have to work so hard to fit in.

Even at home Sal never quite felt relaxed. Despite her demanding job, she still did the lion's share of the housework. Sunday was her most restful day, although she always felt bad that her heavy work schedule meant she couldn't volunteer to do more, and she hardly saw any of the congregation outside of church services.

As she squirmed a little in the management meeting, she consoled herself that it was probably here behind this boardroom desk that she felt she could be herself, more than anywhere else.

Trying to figure out who we are supposed to be is a tough challenge in our segmented life of home, work and church. There's a lot of talk in Hollywood movies and greetings cards that we need to be true to ourselves. But nobody seems to know what that really means. If Jesus is our role model in being glorious and iconic, then as Christians we want to be true to him. But even that is not so simple as it sounds. There are so many different views of who Jesus is.

Think for a moment about your own image of Jesus.[1] Perhaps close your eyes and try to picture him. What does he look like? Where is he? What is he doing? Who is he with? What hand gestures is he using? What is his tone of voice?

Some people automatically imagine the Christmas Card Jesus. Safely snuggled in a manger, gurgling and cooing, Jesus is a safe little baby. He gives a warm, comforting feeling that all is right with the world, and demands very little in return.

Others imagine the Che Guevara-type Jesus. He comes packing a whip, muscles rippling and turning tables over. This Jesus can't be messed with. He's strong and masculine and invincible. He makes you feel powerful, and together you and he are going to change things.

Or there's the BFF[2] Jesus. He is in touch with his feelings. He wants to tell you how much he loves you. He cries at the brokenness of the world and he calls us to weep and feel his pain too.

There's the Ibiza Jesus, who comes with wine on tap. He's the life and soul of the party. He dances. He smiles. He jokes. He calls us to show the world we are having a good time. The better our lives are going and the more fun we are having, the more our friends will want to follow Jesus.

And these are just a few of the popular images connected with Jesus. What about the Hippy Jesus, the Victim Jesus, the Persil-Automatic-Brighter-than-Bright-White Jesus sitting on clouds? Or Jesus hanging on the cross? Or Jesus on Judgment Day?

Each of these pictures of Jesus may portray an element of the truth about who Jesus is, but they are all inadequate in themselves.[3] In fact they are worse than inadequate, because there is a real danger that by focusing on a single aspect of Jesus, it becomes so disproportionate that we end up with a poor caricature. This caricature does more to turn people off Jesus, rather than draw people to him. The Argentinean theologian Renee Padilla argues: "theology in any culture always runs the risk of being... a reduction of the gospel."[4] The South African theologian David Bosch described the way we try to fit Jesus into our lives and values as "an emaciated gospel".[5]

When we edit and embellish our portrayal of Jesus, we not only disfigure and discredit him, we can get distracted from the majestic Christ of the Scriptures.

The apostle Paul is well aware of our ability to effectively pick and choose the Jesus-image we want. In a letter he wrote to a church tempted to adjust their image of Jesus to blend in with the norms of their culture, he attempts a reboot of their imaginations. In a passage reckoned to be one of the most important Christological passages in the New Testament,[6] he attempts to set a new normal for the image of Jesus they see when they close their eyes:

The Son is the image of the invisible God, the firstborn over all creation. For in him all things were created: things in heaven and on earth, visible and invisible, whether thrones or powers or rulers or authorities; all things have been created through him and for him. He is before all things, and in him all things hold together. And he is the head of the body, the church; he is the beginning and the firstborn from among the dead, so that in everything he might have the supremacy. For God was pleased to have all his fullness dwell in him, and through him to reconcile to himself all things, whether things on earth or things in heaven, by making peace through his blood, shed on the cross.[7]

In this remarkable description of Jesus, Paul refuses to let us be content with seeing Jesus as a baby in a manger, a wise sage, a hippy guru, a national mascot, a buddy figure, a political victim, or any other socially acceptable or personally useful portrait. He paints the picture of what theologians call "the cosmic Christ". He is the reason for the existence, the continuing existence and the ultimate culmination of everything.

This was a very countercultural thing to do in a world dominated by the might of the Roman Empire. Husband and wife theologians Brian Walsh and Sylvia Keesmat argue that "in the space of a short well-crafted three stanza poem, Paul subverts every major claim of the [Roman] empire, turning them on their heads, and proclaims Christ to be the Creator, Redeemer and Lord of creation, including the empire."[8] Christianity was seen as such a threat to the Empire that the Romans persecuted Christians ruthlessly.

But despite the dangers of trying to contain a cosmic Christ in words, and the dangers of persecution, Paul does it anyway. He blows up our inadequate images of Jesus by turning the whole thing on its head. It is not that we find a picture of Jesus that suits us and fits into our lives; it is rather that in light of this picture of Jesus' plans for the universe, our lives need to take shape.

Because Jesus is the one in whom all the loose threads of creation past, present and future are woven together, and because he is the inspiration and culmination of everything we do, he can help us connect the dots between our home lives, our working lives and our leisure lives. A true image of Jesus can help us make sense of our identity, wherever we are.

Rebooting our image of Jesus to the default of the cosmic Christ helps us to BE TRUE – true to him and true to his call on our lives. Trying to ensure we see Jesus in all his fullness gives us the true meaning for everything we do, the true purpose for which we exist, the true reason for the story of our lives. He is the organizing principle of the universe and of our lives too.[9]

Being true to who Jesus really is helps us to BE TRUE to who we really are as God's image-bearers. It is in this way that we can learn to become better colleagues, better spouses, better friends and better parents. Being true to who Jesus really is should help us in the big issues surrounding identity as well as helping us in the nitty-gritty decisions of time management, of professional ethics, and of relational integrity.

Sal yawned as the men discussed their golfing day. She was tired of constantly trying to fit in and never succeeding. She rummaged through her bag in an attempt to look distracted. At the bottom she found a card that must have fallen out of her Bible at the weekend. On it were printed some words written by Dietrich Bonhoeffer, the German theologian, from his prison cell in 1944, just a year before he was executed for challenging the Nazi regime. It seemed he struggled with some identity issues of his own:

Who am I? This or the other?
Am I one person today and tomorrow another?
Am I both at once?
A hypocrite before others, and before myself a contemptibly woebegone weakling?
Or is something within me still like a beaten army, fleeing in disorder from victory already achieved?
Who am I?
They mock me, these lonely questions of mine.
Whoever I am, you know, O God, I am yours![10]

For further thought

BE: *reflection*. Meditate on Bonhoeffer's thoughts. Where do you struggle most with fitting in?

SAY: *discussion*. How does rebooting our image of Jesus help give us the integrity to be true to him and true to ourselves?

DO: *action*. What practical thing can you do to remind yourself to be true to Jesus, wherever you are?

CHAPTER 4

BE DOWN TO EARTH

The only sounds on Jim's train that morning were the percussion of wheels on the tracks, the rustle of newspapers and the tinny symphony of fifty iPods playing fifty different songs. He thought back to Sunday morning's sermon, which seemed like half a world away now that he was back in the rhythm of his daily commute.

The preacher had been talking about Jesus entering our world, becoming involved with people, getting his hands dirty. Everyone listening had been encouraged to try to enter someone else's world this week. Ask good questions; show interest; try to walk in someone else's shoes.

But to Jim everyone else's shoes looked pretty shiny this morning. Shinier than his own, even. And as for getting to know people, their ears were blocked – literally, with headphones – and their heads were buried – literally in their laptops or papers. He had prayed with his wife for an opportunity today, but it seemed impossible.

Defeated, Jim quickly retreated back into his own safe and private world and filled his head with the comforting sounds of his favourite band and his mind with the plot of a gripping novel. He felt mildly guilty. He felt slightly annoyed – he was not usually one to be so easily beaten. And he felt slightly discouraged – surely he was made for more than this...

When Jesus entered our world, he didn't come to condemn us to a life of feeling guilty and inadequate, but to rescue us from exactly those things.[1] In order that we could swap guilt and shame for freedom and peace, he swapped the comfort of heaven for hell on earth.[2] Jesus was born into the military oppression of an occupied territory and news of his arrival prompted a mass slaughter of baby boys by an insecure Jewish king. The first Christmas had no smiling snowmen with carrot noses; rather, soldiers with swords and screaming mothers mourning their children.[3]

This is no fairy-tale Christmas scene – there is a very down-to-earth reality of Jesus leaving behind his safe world to come to our dangerous planet. He comes less like a landlord to inspect his property; more like a lifeguard diving to the rescue. This idea is introduced at the beginning of John's gospel and reinforced at its end:

On the evening of that first day of the week, when the disciples were together, with the doors locked for fear of the Jewish leaders, Jesus came and stood among them and said, "Peace be with you!" After he said this, he showed them his hands and side. The disciples were overjoyed when they saw the Lord.

Again Jesus said, "Peace be with you! As the Father has sent me, I am sending you."[4]

Do we really want to be like Jesus, when he came to such a sticky end? I am sure the disciples were thinking along these lines, with images of the crucifixion they had just witnessed fresh in their minds. It's no wonder they bolted the doors in fear. They were next on the hit list. They couldn't possibly fill Jesus' shoes, and did they even want to?

Quieting their fears as he quieted the storm, Jesus enters the room with the word "Peace". *Shalom.*[5] It's so important that

John records Jesus saying it twice. Jesus comforts his disciples, then he gives them the biggest challenge they will ever face and the biggest encouragement they can ever hope for.

Jesus challenges his disciples to BE DOWN TO EARTH like him: "As the Father has sent me, so I send you."

When God the Creator moved into our neighbourhood through the birth of Jesus, he became an ordinary human being just like us. As we have seen, he was sent by the Father not gift-wrapped or bubble-wrapped but in weakness; a defenceless baby born in some back-of-beyond town in a fragile political climate in an occupied, downtrodden nation. As the Father sent Jesus – in weakness into a dangerous world – now Jesus is sending us.

The Latin word for "send" is *missio*, which is where we get our word "mission" from. Theologians call this double-edged mission – in which God the Father sends Jesus into the world and Jesus sends us into the world – the *Missio Dei*, "the mission of God". David Bosch explains that this shows that "mission is not primarily an activity of the church, but an attribute of God. God is a missionary God."[6]

You can imagine the shock of the disciples. They were already fearful that the Jewish rulers or the Roman soldiers would come looking for them and so were hunkering down for an undercover existence. Jesus had different plans. He was sending them out of the bolted door and into the world they were hiding from. If they were scared before, perhaps now they were terrified.

After Jesus challenged them, he encouraged them, and the encouragement was more than enough to meet their fear. It turned them from frightened followers to world-changers. Jesus was sent with the authority of God the Father and with the dynamite presence of the Spirit of God. Not even kings or rulers, storms or soldiers, disaster or disease, nor even death itself could stop Jesus doing the job he had been sent to do. Now he was promising this same authority and power to his disciples. He comforted them. He commissioned them. He anointed them.

Being down to earth does not mean the red-carpet treatment, or a Fast Pass to the ride of our lives. We have to eke out our faith at the coalface of normal existence. Being like Jesus means being weak, finding everyday life an uphill struggle, like most other people around us.

But being down-to-earth Christians also means that we don't just end up in our little corner of the planet with all its challenges by some random accident of nature. We have been sent to our little corner deliberately and with the authority of God. Nothing can stand in our way as we seek to be like Jesus and do the job God has given to us.

What is that job? It is not to attend a prayer meeting every other Wednesday night, or get to the service on time on Sunday. Our job is the same as that of Jesus – to bring the *shalom* peace of God to everybody and every situation.

When we, like the first disciples, feel lacking in confidence and courage, Jesus does not ask us to be super-spiritual, super-busy super-saints. No, he tells us to BE DOWN TO EARTH like he was. Bumping into people at the local watering hole, stopping to chat to people in the street, encouraging those who are frightened, knowing that each appointment is divinely scheduled and a reason to spread a little of God's peace.

Be down to earth...

Jim smiles to himself for beating himself up. Across the carriage someone catches his eye and smiles back. Jim takes off his headphones and says, "Good morning."

It's one small phrase for Jim and one giant peacemaking leap for the kingdom of God. He has momentarily left the comfort of his little world of iPod isolation and made his first step into someone else's.

Jim knows that he is not on that train by accident, but sent by God to be like Jesus. He may be reading the newspaper again, and he hasn't much to tell his wife later tonight, but he has changed. He has his eyes open to what God would have him do next.

Being down to earth is actually quite extraordinary for an ordinary person like Jim.

For further thought

BE: *reflection*. When do you most feel that being a Christian isolates you from other people around you?

SAY: *discussion*. How does the fact that you are "sent" by God challenge and encourage you? Help one another to feel commissioned into your places of work and ministry.

What would you say to someone who said, "I could never be a missionary – I don't like foreign food"?

DO: *action*. How are you going to be a "down to earth" person today?

BE PEACEMAKERS

Lunch box – check. Swim kit – check. Permission slip for school trip – check. Alex felt like a safety engineer clearing a jumbo jet for take-off. Transforming three sleeping children into eager pupils on the next leg of their educative journey to their key stage targets in sixty minutes on a blustery autumn day when only half of the scooters were in working condition, was a feat that would defeat most civil aviation engineers.

As the children spilled into the playground and scattered in opposite directions without so much as a kiss on the cheek, Alex felt the first moral dilemma of the day approaching. She looked at the two groups of parents in the playground divided by an invisible Berlin Wall surrounded by social mines and barbed taboo-wire and a definite no woman's land in the middle.

Alex had friends in both groups, so whichever group she chose to associate with this morning would be seen as a definite snub to somebody, as she knew from experience. She had only a few seconds to decide as she strode across the playground. Who should she be today?

Life is full of social divisions. With those divisions come decisions. How should we fly – first class or economy class?

Where should we shop – Waitrose or Lidl? Where should we live – urban or rural? Even postcodes say something about us – SW1 or E17? Whether it is where to stand in a playground, or what we choose to wear, or who to chat to at work, we cannot escape the fact that the divided world we live in influences most things we do.

BE PEACEMAKERS. This sounds like such a serene description of Christian living. However, the reality is that it is actually a serious and dangerous conscription into situations of conflict.

Being peacemakers was no easier in the ancient world, where divisions were also clearly defined. In the Roman world of that day, slaves and masters lived in close proximity to one another and yet were worlds apart socially. In Jewish circles men didn't talk to women in public, and weren't even allowed to sit next to them at the synagogue. Men's daily prayers included an expression of gratitude that God had not made them a woman or a Gentile.[1] If a Jewish boy dared to marry a non-Jewish girl in some communities, it was not a wedding that was planned, but a funeral.[2] Even the design of the temple in Jerusalem contained a clear demarcation between the place where Jews could go and the space for everyone else. The "Court of the Gentiles" ran all the way around the temple, so that they could see it but were very aware that they could not come into it. And there were warning signs in Greek and Latin that, according to John Stott, read, "in effect, not 'Trespassers will be prosecuted'; but 'Trespassers will be executed'."[3]

It is into this context that Paul writes his letter to the church in Ephesus:

Therefore, remember that formerly you who are Gentiles by birth and called "uncircumcised" by those who call themselves "the circumcision" (which is done in the body by human hands) – remember that at that time you were separate from Christ, excluded from citizenship in Israel and foreigners to the covenants of the promise, without hope and without God in the world. But now in Christ Jesus you who once were far away have been brought near through the blood of Christ.

For he himself is our peace, who has made the two one and has destroyed the barrier, the dividing wall of hostility, by setting aside in his flesh the law with its commands and regulations. His purpose was to create in himself one new humanity out of the two, thus making peace, and in one body to reconcile both of them to God through the cross, by which he put to death their hostility. He came and preached peace to you who were far away and peace to those who were near. For through him we both have access to the Father by one Spirit.[4]

At the moment that Jesus died on the cross, the curtain in the temple that divided the most holy place from the rest of the temple was torn in two from top to bottom. This powerful visual aid demonstrated that God was opening the way to bring peace between us and him, and offering access into his presence. Paul's argument in Ephesians takes this one step further, arguing that when Jesus died he also effectively nuked the wall that separated the Jews from the Gentiles. Jesus, the ultimate Peacemaker, created not only peace between us and God through his death, but also peace between us and other people.[5]

I remember as a teenager watching the euphoric scenes when the wall that divided East and West Berlin was taken down. There was cheering as chisels, sledgehammers and bulldozers smashed down the wall that had divided two halves of one city, two ideologies, and thousands of families. Crowds on both sides scrambled over the rubble to embrace each other as tears and cheers mingled together. This is the picture of reconciliation that I associate with the destruction that Jesus brought to ethnic divisions in our world.

Paul is encouraging the ethnically diverse church in Ephesus to live out the reality of this destroyed wall between Jews and Gentiles by celebrating their unity, and putting an end to isolation and separation and divisions and conflicts.

Later in the letter he calls the Ephesian Christians to "Make every effort to keep the unity of the Spirit through the bond of peace."[6] Those words are included in Scripture because they apply to us. Peace between us and God is to be lived out in our lives, in our churches and in our world. We are the ones drafted to the task of peacemaking, bridging the gap where there is division, enabling access where there is separation, and facilitating conversation where there is conflict.

Jesus himself said, "Blessed are the peacemakers, for they will be called the children of God."[7] The verse comes right before the one that says, "Blessed are those who are persecuted". Peacemaking is no easy calling. Standing in no man's land is likely to see us getting shot at from both sides. But peacemaking is a family trait. This is the way people will know that we are children of God.

I have met some Christians who, in their call to be peacemakers, have left comfortable jobs to work in war-torn countries like Sudan or Congo. Others are seeking to bridge the gap between the homed and the homeless, the well and the sick, the well off and the downtrodden. Others are working to break down the barriers that separate different age groups[8] or racial groups or social groups within their churches, workplaces and streets.

Today's challenge is to be peacemakers, wherever we are and for the rest of our lives, until one day our job will be finished and Jesus will be finally revealed as the Prince of Peace.

Alex hesitates in the playground and then decides to take up a position in the demilitarized zone between the two factions. She wonders if she is appearing stand-offish to everyone and tries to compensate with an extra-enthusiastic smile.

If anyone catches her eye, she is going to be very relieved. Also she is quite determined to capitalize on it and invite that person back for a coffee.

She waits there a long time. She wonders if she will be standing there for five minutes or five weeks or five years.

For further thought

BE: *reflection*. When have you felt most connected to Jesus as a peacemaker? When have you experienced peace and facilitated peace?

SAY: *discussion*. List the situations of conflict and separation where you live and work. Pray into those situations and come up with some strategies for being a peacemaker.

DO: *action*. Choose one of the situations of conflict discussed above and think how you could be a peacemaker or bring a peace offering today to bridge the division.

CHAPTER 6

BE UNSHAKEABLE

Monday, 4 p.m.

As Gemma's feet pounded the streets, she felt good. After several months of training, she no longer found every step torture. Her heart was not bursting out of her chest, her shins and knees did not ache for two days after each run. All that money she had invested in new running shoes and Lycra and fitness apps had paid off.

Now she could get fit, stay trim and get the space she needed in her life to reflect and pray a little. Gemma even felt that she was experiencing a new level of intimacy with God that reminded her of the early days of her faith.

But she knew that she had been here before. Once it was the cold winter months that had sapped all her enthusiasm. Once an injury had set her back. For several years she had had a job with long hours. And once it was a relationship breakdown that literally stopped her in her tracks. Was it going to be different this time?

There are many things in my life that I can't quit, no matter how hard I try. Usually they are unhealthy, selfish or stupid habits that I know are going to cause me problems down the road. There are many other things in my life that I can't stick with, no matter how hard I try. Usually they are the important, healthy and vital parts of my life. This topsy-turvy problem means that while I can invariably manage to find time to nip into McDonald's on my way home from work, I very rarely make our church prayer meetings. While I have never forgotten to turn the TV on for the latest episode of *Dr Who*, I have occasionally missed assemblies and concerts my children have invited me to. I have stuck with the same football team for thirty years, but in the same time frame I have moved jobs, homes and churches more times than I care to count.

Sticking with one church for the long haul is hard for many of us, but there are many more who find they can't even stick with Christianity. Statistically, the church in the UK has a greater rate of loss than the *Titanic*. Over 70 per cent of our young people do not see their faith survive into adulthood.[1] This is part of a global problem. Church leaders in Africa, Asia and America report a similar dropout of Christians in their twenties. But this abandonment of faith and church is not restricted to young adults. Sadly, I know many Christians who served God faithfully for up to half a century before quitting. Some have turned their backs on seemingly successful ministries and still others have walked out on faithful spouses. Of those that are left, there is a whole group who are still turning up to church services, singing the songs and enduring the sermons, but although their bodies are in the gatherings their hearts are not in it any more.

We know that Jesus persevered to the end, but he was the sinless Son of God and Saviour of the World. How can we BE UNSHAKEABLE and unwavering like Jesus was?

The whole book of Hebrews was written to deter Christians from giving up and includes grave warnings of what happens to those who either drift away or determine to leave the faith. But in chapter 12 the writer moves from warning to inspiration:

Therefore, since we are surrounded by such a great cloud of witnesses, let us throw off everything that hinders and the sin that so easily entangles. And let us run with perseverance the race marked out for us, fixing our eyes on Jesus, the pioneer and perfecter of faith. For the joy set before him endured the cross, scorning its shame, and sat down at the right hand of the throne of God. Consider him who endured such opposition from sinners, so that you will not grow weary and lose heart.[2]

The sprint may be a metaphor for our times. We like quick returns on investment, speed-reading, fast food, drop-a-dress-size-in-a-month, instant access, and overnight sensations. As James Gleik writes:

instantaneity rules... instant coffee, instant intimacy, instant replay and instant gratification. Pollers use electronic devices during political speeches to measure opinions on the wing, before they have been fully formed... fast-food restaurants add express lanes. If we do not understand time, we become its victims.[3]

Harder, better, faster are watchwords of our day.[4] But the running metaphor that is described in the verses above is not a mad dash, or a 100-metre sprint. It is an endurance race.

According to this passage, the secret to our resilience is remembering the endurance of Jesus. He not only saw his own mission on earth to its gruesome end on the cross, but he is also both the author and perfecter of our faith. He's started, so he'll finish.

In some translations Jesus is described here as the "pacesetter"[5] or "trailblazer" for our faith. He is the one who goes with us and the one who has gone ahead of us, showing us how to run, and more importantly, how to run to the end. Jesus' motivation was joy. The joy of pleasing God, the joy of completing his mission, and the joy of rescuing humanity enabled his unshakeable resolve to endure the shame and the pain of the cross. This joy saw him through the terrible isolation in which he was abandoned by his friends, rejected by the crowds, disconnected from his heavenly Father.

Many athletes are inspired by picturing themselves crossing that finish line and standing on the podium listening to the applause of the crowds, and this helps them to dig deep during their years of painful training and preparation. The writer to the Hebrews asks us to make Jesus that fixed point, our goal and our hope. No matter what life throws at us, no matter what distracts us – one day we will be with Jesus at the finish line. Remaining true to Jesus and remaining inspired by him helps us to BE UNSHAKEABLE.[6]

Fixing our eyes on Jesus is easy when we begin. Like someone who has just fallen in love, there is often an initial irrepressible enthusiasm, but sadly, the initial passion doesn't last for ever; either it matures into a deep love and commitment, or it bows out or fades away.

The verses above offer us two pieces of practical advice to enable us to keep it up for the long haul and reach that maturity. First, for us to BE UNSHAKEABLE, we need to shake off anything that hinders or distracts us. Whatever takes our eyes off Jesus needs to be recognized as superfluous and dealt with as soon as possible, before it has the chance to turn us into quitters.

Secondly, for us to BE UNSHAKEABLE, we also need to be shaken into action by the "great crowd of witnesses" spurring us on. The writer is referring back to the heroes of the faith, named and unnamed, in chapter 11, as well as the supportive church mentioned in chapter 10: "not giving up meeting together... but encouraging one another" (verse 25). Our pursuit of Jesus is to be encouraged by reflecting on the lives of those who have run before us and those who run with us.

When the going gets tough in our faith, many Christians quit church. That is the time when we most need the help of other believers. When we are tempted to quit our faith, it is even more important to commit ourselves to sticking close to the church. I am not a very able runner, but when I do run, I run best with friends. The longest run I have ever managed was due in large part to a friend who committed to sticking with me, however far I lagged behind the rest of the running pack. Maybe there are people you know who need your company as they struggle to follow Jesus, their pacesetter. Maybe you are lagging behind. Is there someone you can ask to run with you as you pursue Jesus?

Back home, Gemma is not sitting down. She has made some decisions during her run and she is going to put them in place quickly before her enthusiasm wanes or is eclipsed by the practicalities of her lifestyle. She opens her computer on her kitchen worktop and signs up to a local 10K race for charity as she downs a couple of glasses of water. She emails a few friends to see if they will join her.

Two minutes is all it takes to help keep her on track physically for the next few months. On her next run she will work out what the equivalent decisions are to maintain her spiritual life.

For further thought

DO: *action*. What can you do practically to ensure you remain unshakeable in your faith?

SAY: *discussion*. How does Jesus being our trailblazer, running ahead of us, and our pacesetter, running beside us, help us keep going when we are tempted to give up? At the end of Jesus' endurance race, he "sat down at the right hand of the throne of God". How does this promise of rest help us shake off all distractions?

BE: *reflection.* Read, meditate on and memorize Acts 2:25–26 in light of the Hebrews passage above:

> *I saw the Lord always before me.*
> *Because he is at my right hand,*
> *I will not be shaken.*
> *Therefore my heart is glad and my tongue rejoices;*
> *my body also will rest in hope.*

CHAPTER 7

BE AVAILABLE

Tuesday, 2.30 p.m.

No time for lunch. The board meeting had run over, and Celia's iPhone now told her that there were 95 unanswered emails in her inbox and three missed calls she had to return before the next meeting. "Find me the best way to get to Edinburgh by 6 p.m. tomorrow!" she barked at her Personal Assistant as she sped on to Meeting Room 4. As she entered the room the hubbub of conversation instantly stopped. She said, "Let's get down to business…"

Two hours later Celia was in a taxi speeding to the station. At last, five minutes to skim through those emails. By the time she was home, she had almost cleared her bulging inbox, written a report and booked the next day's train tickets.

As she walked in the door of her immaculate but silent flat, she paused: although she had been in contact with over fifty people that day, she did not know a thing about their lives.

We live in strange days. At one level we are better connected than ever before. Thanks to texting, Skyping, instant messaging, social media and our ever-evolving, ever-present mobile phones, we can receive a steady stream of world news, stay in touch with acquaintances that we would have lost track of, and are contactable almost anywhere in the world at any time in the day. Perhaps through our technology we are attempting to be both omnipresent and omniscient.[1] In other words, many of us like to think we can be everywhere and know everything. But ironically, this "always on" culture can mean we are actually less available to the people around us. It is not unusual to see people tripping over as they walk down the street because their eyes are glued to their smart phone. Or to notice people zoning out of conversations to check Facebook or Twitter. Or to observe children sitting on a bus in an eerie silence, all playing the latest game on their iPods.[2]

Perhaps we can learn something from the Jesus who is both truly omnipresent and yet fully available to all of us. God first explained this to an ordinary small-town carpenter who was trying to work out if his fiancée had cheated on him, and whether to break off the engagement:

> But after he had considered this, an angel of the Lord appeared to him in a dream and said, "Joseph son of David, do not be afraid to take Mary home as your wife, because what is conceived in her is from the Holy Spirit. She will give birth to a son, and you are to give him the name Jesus, because he will save his people from their sins."
>
> All this took place to fulfil what the Lord had said through the prophet: "The virgin will conceive and give birth to a son, and they will call him Immanuel" (which means "God with us").[3]

Before Jesus was even born, he was being introduced as "Immanuel", "God with us". The significance of this title was underlined by the fact that, for centuries, this was who was promised to come to Israel's rescue. God would be with his beleaguered people. But Matthew connects this ancient longing with the events he witnessed in his day. This introduction to his gospel is mirrored in his conclusion, as he ends with Jesus' promise to be "God with us" even "to the very end of the age".[4]

Joseph was in an awkward position; so were the disciples. Both felt that the world was watching and judging them. But

God had not abandoned them. God wanted them to know very clearly that he was present and available.

In fact, Jesus' whole life was a riff on this theme. Wherever he went he made time for people, listened to them, engaged them, turned their lives upside down. As we shall see, even when he attempted to take time out with his disciples and the crowds followed him, he refused to deny them access. Whether it was the crowds, the lepers, the tax collectors, the women, the children, the disabled, the sick or the troubled, he took time to be with them. Never mind that in his society these kinds of people should not have been seen or heard; Jesus would break every socially dividing taboo to see and hear them. He ate with sinners, he spoke to women, he listened to children, he even healed Gentiles. Jesus was "God with us all".

And so at the end of the gospel of Matthew, just before he ascends into heaven, Jesus promises that his available presence is not limited by geography or chronology: he is still with us to the ends of the earth and until the end of the earth.

This is an amazing promise. Wherever we go, we have been commissioned by Jesus and we are accompanied by Jesus. If we go with a parent to hear results from a medical test, or accompany a child to a disciplinary meeting, or go to court to support a loved one – Christ is with us. As we talk to a passer-by at the bus stop, or listen to a neighbour's troubles, Christ is with us. As we enter those cultural no-go areas and take risks to help others come to know the grace of our God – Christ is with us.

Being like Jesus means learning this skill of being present. It means learning to make eye contact with cashiers at the supermarket, trying to engage the taxi driver in conversation, properly listening to the chatter of the hairdresser. It means prioritizing the needs of those in need around us, and risking the disapproval of friends to help strangers.

Some would say being available means getting unplugged from our gadgets, but this is not necessarily the case. Sometimes we need to switch off to be switched on to the people in the same room as us. And sometimes we can use our gadgets to be the listening ear or the helpful friend or the distant encourager.[5] Sometimes our gadgets can help us to access information that will help us understand the needs of people all around the world and encourage and advocate for them.

Fixing our eyes on Jesus, as we thought about in the previous chapter, does not mean we close our eyes to the needs of people around us. Shaking off unhelpful distractions to our faith does not mean we refuse to be distracted by the cries for help that seem to slow us down in our fast-paced lives. Being unshakeable and being available go together because being present for others reflects the fact that Jesus was present for others.

I once had the privilege of meeting a man who wanted to BE AVAILABLE to lonely young men facing extreme pressures. Captain Lee is a chaplain in the Korean army. His parish includes the demilitarized zone that separates communist North Korea from democratic South Korea. He knows that the young conscripts (aged nineteen or twenty) doing their military service in this dangerous area often suffer from severe loneliness and depression. Every year many of them end their lives with the automatic weapons issued to them. The long watch through the night is the time when they feel most vulnerable, and so Captain Lee deliberately pays his pastoral visits in the middle of the night, taking them hot coffee and tea in the winter and cold coffee and tea in the summer. Through the offer of a drink, a friendly smile and a listening ear he lets these lonely press-ganged soldiers experience the presence of Jesus, Immanuel, God with us.[6]

Perhaps we can identify with the role of unofficial and secret chaplains. We can be the means by which our neighbours, colleagues, friends and family can come to experience the presence of God. We will never be omnipresent like Jesus, however much we try, but we can learn from Jesus, Immanuel, to BE AVAILABLE.

Celia put her feet up in her quiet house. She thought about sending a tweet apologizing for being too busy to stop and ask how people were. But then she stopped. It wasn't quite personal enough.

So she texted a few people individually and waited for them to respond. Then she asked God for forgiveness for ignoring him today too, and thanked him for his presence with her.

As her mind wandered into tomorrow's busy schedule, she wondered how she could become a little more available.

For further thought

BE: *reflection*. Think of all the people you will encounter/have encountered today. What are their needs? How available are you to them?

SAY: *discussion*. Why is it hard for Celia to be available to her colleagues and employees? Why is it hard for us sometimes to be available?

Who around us in our communities would benefit most from a listening ear, a shoulder to lean on, or a friend? How could your church make itself more available to the vulnerable in your community?

DO: *action*. Look through your diary. Do you need to find more space or fill more space in order to become more available to others?

CHAPTER 8

BE DESCENDANTS

He had been waiting to have the conversation for a few days now. With the kids safely tucked up in bed, they stood in the kitchen making packed lunches together for the week ahead.

James had rehearsed some possible ways he could introduce the topic: "There's an opportunity that's come up at work." But that sounded like it was all about him. "There's an opportunity for our family to have a whole new lifestyle." This was better, but sounded a bit like a sales pitch. "Dubai is a very wealthy country but a spiritual and literal desert" – possibly James over-egged the sandwich and the pitch on that one.

He decided to just dive in: "Darling, I've been offered a promotion at work. It's a lot more money but it means a relocation to Dubai to look after the whole Middle East region."

After a long pause Gemma burst into tears, dropping the remaining egg mayonnaise on the floor. He thought she was saying, between the sobs, "I am so happy for you, but I feel so settled here."

This was a once-in-a-lifetime career opportunity and he knew he could give his family a better lifestyle out there. But he only had one family and he didn't want to mess it up. Who was he supposed to be in this situation – leader, provider, risk-taker, sacrificer?

With only a week to make this massive decision, he was in for some sleepless nights.

Living like Jesus, as his followers and spiritual descendants, influences all our decisions, whether they are the big career and family choices, or the everyday selections of where to go, who to speak to, how to react, or whether to intervene.

But Jesus was a "descend-ant" in another sense of the word – he came down, descended, to our level, and stooped to serve us. The incredibly humble and downwardly mobile attitude of Jesus challenges our dreams, ambitions and decisions. In the following song Paul challenges the believers in Philippi to reflect on the life trajectory of Jesus, not just for their emotional stimulation, but also to help them be more like Jesus and reboot the motivations that drive their lives:

Do nothing out of selfish ambition or vain conceit. Rather, in humility value others above yourselves, not looking to your own interests but each of you to the interests of the others.

In your relationships with one another, have the same attitude of mind Christ Jesus had:

Who, being in very nature God,
did not consider equality with God something to be
used to his own advantage;
rather, he made himself nothing
by taking the very nature of a servant,
being made in human likeness.
And being found in appearance as a human being,
he humbled himself
by becoming obedient to death –
even death on a cross!
Therefore God exalted him to the highest place
and gave him the name that is above every name,
that at the name of Jesus every knee should bow,
in heaven and on earth and under the earth,

and every tongue acknowledge that Jesus Christ is Lord,
to the glory of God the Father.[1]

Paul is probably quoting one of the oldest Christian hymns.[2] This ancient song tracks the life of Jesus: his birth, life, death, resurrection, ascension and glorification. Paul asks us to consider the attitudes that drove Jesus. He chose not to hold on to the honour, majesty, power, position and privilege that were rightly his, choosing instead to live in poverty and squalor. He not only descended from heaven to earth, but chose the entry level of a servant and the exit level of a condemned and executed criminal.

Paul makes a clear link between who Jesus is, what he did and why, and who we are called to be, and what we are called to do. His inescapable challenge is: "Do nothing out of selfish ambition."

Every aspect of our lives is covered by this prohibition. Whether at home or in business, as an individual or as part of a church, whether publicly or privately, we are to do nothing out of selfish ambition. Instead, as descendants of Jesus, we are to BE DESCENDANTS – downwardly mobile, humble servants, like Jesus.

The Author of Life wrote himself into the pages of our history by being born and mistreated as a created human being, and dying for the sins of the world. Not one of us can repeat what he did. But we can emulate the attitude that shaped his choices.

Christian history is littered with stories of men and women who saw the needs of others and took the hard route of humble, sacrificial service. Many of their stories are lost. Some seem insignificant. But for every story preserved, there are many more men and women who put the needs of elderly relatives ahead of their own, sacrificing time, career or status to help them. There are many parents who forgo their own dreams and ambitions to care for sick or needy children. There are many employees who forgo promotion to be able to better serve their community. There are many Christians who, in their working lives, serve God by daily putting the needs of others ahead of their own in sacrificial service.

In 1732 at a prayer meeting in Germany, the tragic tale of Anthony Ulrich was shared. He had been kidnapped from Africa and taken to the Danish-controlled island of St Thomas in the West Indies to be a slave. The conditions he and thousands of other slaves were facing moved many in that prayer meeting to tears. One of the intercessors that night was Leonard, and he, with his friend Nitschmann, decided to go to St Thomas to serve as missionaries.

The two men walked to Copenhagen to ask permission to travel and were asked the customary questions about how they would make a living. Nitschmann told the King's Chamberlain: "We shall work as slaves among the slaves,"[3] to which the Chamberlain replied, "If you go on like that, you will stand your ground the wide world over." These two young men offered to leave behind the power and prestige of free European men, to experience life alongside the dispossessed slaves of West Africa. They were willing to swap comfort for torture and freedom for captivity. They were willing to let the needs of others direct the trajectory of their lives.

Thirteen thousand slaves became baptized followers of Christ in St Thomas due to the willingness of Leonard and Nitschmann to sell themselves into slavery for the chance to show others the grace of God.

Four hundred miles away is another country populated by the descendants of kidnapped African slaves. As the people of Haiti were rebuilding their community following the catastrophic force 7 earthquake of 2010, which killed 230,001 people,[4] I had the privilege of meeting three beautiful bright-eyed Haitian children living in poverty in Port-au-Prince. I asked them about their dreams for the future, and the answers I received challenged me at every level. Aged eight, they are already on a descendant trajectory, allowing their decisions to be shaped by Jesus, putting others' needs ahead of their own. They are making choices so that one day they can be the effective gynaecologists, structural engineers and paramedics that their country needs.

Those three children have something to teach all of us. If to be a descendant of Jesus and to BE DESCENDANTS like Jesus had an impact on who we all chose to be in life, then our world would be a different place.

James knew the job opportunity was good for him and his career, but ringing in his ears were the words, "Do nothing out of selfish ambition." As he looked at his wife he thought about how the move would affect her. There would be no need to make packed lunches on his new salary, but then again, he would be dragging her away from her friends and family and everything familiar. He thought he knew which way he should go for the greatest collateral good.

For further thought

BE: *reflection*. Consider your own ambitions and dreams. To what extent are they influenced by our society's values, by selfish motives, or by a desire to serve God and his world?

SAY: *discussion*. How would you counsel James and/or James's wife as they struggle to make their decision? How could a "descendant trajectory" affect where you end up in five or ten years' time?

DO: *action*. Try to go the extra mile in something small today to practise being descendants like Jesus, putting others' needs above your own.

CHAPTER 9

BE GO-BETWEENS

Thursday, 6.45 a.m.

Jaina reluctantly crept out of bed and stealthily got ready for the day ahead. She cursed the kettle for making too much noise and then impatiently downed the hot coffee. As she waited for the caffeine to kick-start her day, her stomach began to burn. Was it the coffee or the sense of dread about going back into the office?

At least she only worked part time – the past two days had felt like an oasis of peace, despite the school runs, the trip to the supermarket and the church business meeting. Now she was heading back to the war zone that was her office.

The company was feeling the impact of "quantitative easing" and was having to downsize, and so everyone was fighting for job survival. Senior management wanted everyone to work longer hours with a pay freeze, and it was making life intolerable, especially for the part-timers.

Colleagues she used to think were friends were using underhand tactics to position themselves to avoid the cuts. One of the other Christians was receiving some particularly vicious harassment, and she was glad she had always kept her faith private.

She would have loved to have crawled back into bed, but instead she braced herself for another day at the office.

I often think of myself as a go-between. My work means I am constantly going between different cities, different churches, different countries. I go between home and work so many times a week that I have been known to take my inbox to the dinner table, and to end a phone call to a colleague with the "Love you" usually reserved for my immediate family members!

My children are also coaching me to be a go-between. With an average of five kids[1] getting under each other's feet from breakfast to supper and beyond, there are plenty of quarrels and dilemmas to be intercepted by a go-between father-in-training. "But Mummy said it was OK!" "Dad, make my brother give me the remote control!"

As Christians we are also called to BE GO-BETWEENS in the spiritual sense, as Jesus was. The writer to the Hebrews explains it like this:

> *Therefore, since we have a great high priest who has ascended into heaven, Jesus the Son of God, let us hold firmly to the faith we profess. For we do not have a high priest who is unable to empathize with our weaknesses, but we have one who has been tempted in every way, just as we are – yet he did not sin. Let us then approach God's throne of grace with confidence, so that we may receive mercy and find grace to help us in our time of need.*[2]

The book of Hebrews was written for Christians who were in a battle zone. Many were reeling from the pain of divided families and facing persecution from the state.[3] Loyalties were being stretched as brothers and sisters, sons and daughters, neighbours and friends were converting to following Jesus. As the New Testament scholar William Lane says, the letter was "addressed to a group of Christians who were experiencing a crisis of faith and a failure of nerve."[4] There was a lot to lose for these converts. They faced being insulted in public, having their property confiscated, being shunned by their relatives, imprisonment, physical beatings and even execution. For some, the sacrifices felt too great. These verses were written to encourage them to be unshakeable by reminding them of their identity as go-betweens.

These verses provided a helpful analogy for those who found themselves torn between Judaism and Christianity. At the hands of the Jewish authorities, they were being mocked and persecuted for betraying their history and scriptures and priests. At the hands of the Gentiles, they were being persecuted for their cultural Jewish roots. And so this letter, soaked in Old Testament references, showed them how Jesus bridged the gap – by fulfilling history, by embodying the temple, and most importantly, by being the perfect High Priest.[5]

The role of the High Priest in Jewish tradition was that of the supreme go-between, mediating between God and the people. He was the one who would enter God's holy presence on behalf of the people and offer sacrifices to atone for sins.

Jesus is the perfect High Priest because, unlike the Levitical priests,[6] he was without sin. He also understands us perfectly, having lived with us and like us. And he knows God perfectly, having "gone through the heavens" to sit at God's right hand.

Knowing that Jesus sympathizes with us in our pain, struggles, temptations and persecutions is both a source of comfort and a source of encouragement to keep going. Because he advocates for us, we are enabled to access God ourselves with confidence.

Not only are we offered grace and mercy for ourselves at God's throne, but also we are invited into God's presence to advocate for others. We too are to BE GO-BETWEENS, like Jesus.

These twin roles of Jesus' priesthood as sympathizer and intercessor shape our calling too. Peter explains it, saying that we, as God's people, are "a royal priesthood".[7] Like Jesus, we too are called to be sympathizers and mediators.

Being sympathizers involves feeling the pain, distress, injustice and temptation of the people with whom we share our lives and our planet, sometimes facing those problems ourselves, just as our great High Priest did.

Being mediators involves using our prayers, our lives and our words to intercede for those around us, pleading for them before God, and pleading on God's behalf to them. We stand in the doorway in order to connect God with people and people with God, providing access, facilitating relationship. As the church, we are the halfway house between the brokenness of the world and the perfection of the coming Kingdom.

Being a Jesus-like go-between is a high calling indeed. Introducing people to God and helping them access the Creator of the World is an amazing privilege that we can share with our Lord and Saviour. Every time we sympathize with someone in their pain, or advocate for the vulnerable, or offer grace where it is undeserved, or practically help someone in need, we fulfil our identity as priests in the world.

Jaina survived another day at the office and came home with her mind stewing over the frustrations of the day. On top of this, she felt confused. The other Christian in the office had accosted her and told her that while he had been praying, he had felt God provoke him to challenge Jaina: "If you are really a Christian, perhaps you should stop hiding it, however difficult the consequences."

He wanted her to begin to pray for their colleagues, for their company. Perhaps together they could somehow make a difference, he said.

How badly did she need her job? How badly did she need to feel accepted? What should she do?

For further thought

BE: *reflection*. When do you feel the weakest with regard to resisting sin and temptation and coping with suspicion and mistreatment because of your faith? How does Hebrews 4:14–16 speak to you in those situations?

SAY: *discussion*. Jesus identified with us in our need and now speaks on our behalf in front of God. Who are the people that don't know God that you identify most closely with? What does it mean for you to be priest for them?

What would you do in Jaina's shoes?

DO: *action*. In the circles that you move in, who are the people that most need someone to speak up for them? How can you be their advocate?

CHAPTER 10

BE LUMINOUS

The board meeting seemed to be going on forever. Taking minutes had never been Hope's favourite part of her job. But with the Friday afternoon feeling, the stuffiness of the boardroom and the fine detail of the annual accounts, she was struggling to stay awake. She wasn't alone – half of the board members were either on the edge of dozing off or distractedly tapping away at their laptops and smart phones.

It was a great day to bury bad news. The CEO skipped over section 7.1 of the agenda. She glanced to see what had been missed, and it was a follow-up to a question raised at the last meeting about "conflict of interest with contractors". Everyone knew that the boss had used her brother-in-law's firm to handle some rebuilding work. Everyone, that is, except the board members. And it looked like they were not going to find out.

Nobody had noticed the omission except Hope, but there was an unwritten rule that administrative staff were to be silent members in board meetings. Hope's job was to record and not to comment. She heard her mother's advice in the back of her mind: "Keep your head down, work hard and avoid trouble."

The CEO paused after asking the hopefully hypothetical question: "Any other business?" Ten seconds, and Hope knew the board members would be out the door, leaving her to turn the lights out, email the minutes and get on her way home for the weekend, unless...

Every year as winter comes and my evening cycle ride home gets darker and darker, I always find myself asking the same question: "Why didn't I buy a better light for my bike?" Hurtling down those unlit rural B-roads with motorists zooming past me, I am all too aware that my entire life is dependent on one tiny little red LED light fixed behind my saddle. I can't go any faster, because my front light isn't great either and I can't see far enough ahead. So I power on at average speed through the darkness until, finally, I approach the glowing town ahead of me. It makes me wonder what life would be like if I was always in the dark.

Perhaps the disciples were wondering the same thing when they encountered a man born blind. His disability prompted them to ask one of the most difficult questions anyone can ever ask: "Why do innocent people suffer?" They couldn't have asked a better person. If anyone could answer this question, it was the Creator and Sustainer of the universe. Would he shine some light on this difficult issue?

> *As he went along, he saw a man blind from birth. His disciples asked him, "Rabbi, who sinned, this man or his parents, that he was born blind?"*
>
> *"Neither this man nor his parents sinned," said Jesus, "but this happened so that the works of God might be displayed in him. As long as it is day, we must do the works of him who sent me. Night is coming, when no one can work. While I am in the world, I am the light of the world."*[1]

Jesus first debunks the disciples' assumptions. The man was not blind because he or his parents did something terrible. The Bible consistently teaches that although suffering is a consequence of sin in the world, it is very rarely the direct consequence of personal or familial sin.[2] Jesus then goes on to give his dangerous, world-shaking answer.

The suffering that this blind man was experiencing was an opportunity for the glory of God to be shown. His life was a stage set for God to shine on. This is not a full and watertight answer to the problem of suffering, but it is a fresh perspective that should be life-changing. Our suffering and that of others can be an opportunity for God's glory to shine. We need to totally reconfigure our mindset: God does not exist to give *us* the chance to be or see better – no, we exist to give *God* the chance to be better seen.[3]

Jesus speaks with urgency, culminating in the incredible claim: "I am the light of the world." Not only do we exist so that God can be better seen, but Jesus existed on earth so that he could make God visible as he shone with God's compassion and grace and mercy.

Jesus is perfectly luminous, helping people to see God's goodness in the context of a broken world. We too are called to BE LUMINOUS in the same way:

> *You are the light of the world. A town built on a hill cannot be hidden. Neither do people light a lamp and put it under a bowl. Instead they put it on its stand, and it gives light to everyone in the house. In the same way, let your light shine before others, that they may see your good deeds and glorify your Father in heaven.*[4]

It was incredible enough for Jesus to make the bold statement, "I am the light of the world." With just a few words he was claiming to be the I AM Yahweh God who revealed himself to Moses in Exodus, and he was claiming to be able to banish the darkness and suffering and sin of the entire planet. To then go on and call us to be the light of the world was even more incredible. We are to be like Jesus, revealing God and banishing darkness.

My bike lights may not shine very brightly, but on those dark country roads a little bit of light goes a long way. The same principle is at work in our lives. We may not feel that we are the light of the world. We may look at ourselves and feel we do not shine at all. But put us in a dark place, and whatever little radiance we have suddenly stands out a mile.

There are plenty of dark places around us, from the relationship breakdown across the road, to the evasion of truth in a board meeting, to the shady side of politics, professional sports or public policy. I have heard Christians say that they have no interest in politics, or would not choose to work in banking, because those professions are too dirty or too dark. Similarly, I have heard Christians complain long and hard about the state of family life, or the corruption of our schools or hospitals. But bemoaning these is, in one sense, like cursing the night for being dark. We are not supposed to criticize from afar, or run from darkness. As the church, it is our job to go into those places to be luminous and shine as the light of the world.

My local school was a dark place. There was plenty of bullying, racism, disrespect and all sorts of broken lives. One morning in a chemistry lab something was lit up, but it was not a Bunsen burner. It was Steve, a brand-new Christian convert from the night before, standing up and inviting us all to join him on his new journey. Thanks to a prayerful mother, a kindly Sunday school teacher and some diligent schools workers, chinks of light were already breaking into my mind and heart. But that morning, through Steve's brave words, the lights were turned on for me.

Since that day I have seen many Christians bring light to dark places. I have seen Christian foster carers offering light and hope to struggling teenagers, Christian politicians bringing God's justice into thorny political debates, Christian bankers taking a tough stand in a boardroom, Christian advertising creatives using their influence to help fight body-image manipulation, and too many more to mention. It is in these dark places that we shine as the light of the world.

When I am cycling down the pitch-black roads near my

home, I am especially grateful when the stars come out. They may look like tiny pinpricks of light but they have made a huge difference to me on many occasions. I am even more grateful for the myriad Christians who have shone in the darkness, setting an example for me, making the world we live in a better place and pointing many people towards our heavenly Father.[5]

It was as Hope visualized walking out of the door and turning off the lights late that Friday afternoon that she realized that she had a responsibility not to keep the board members in the dark about the controversial conflict of interests. After all, she was God's light in her workplace, however dim she felt.

Before she could change her mind, she felt herself clearing her throat and then saying the words, "Just checking for the minutes that we covered everything in section 7."

Her CEO visibly changed colour twice: first all the blood rushed from her face and then it all rushed back again with double the intensity. She had been rumbled and she knew it. No amount of fumbling with papers was going to help her.

Hope knew what she was doing, but did not know how things would end up. "Lord, make my life a place where your light is seen, whatever it costs me," she silently prayed.

For further thought

BE: *reflection*. How do you react to the statement, "God does not exist to give *us* the chance to be or see better – no, we exist to give *God* the chance to be better seen"?

SAY: *discussion*. What would you say to someone who said: "Suffering happens to us because of unconfessed sin in our lives or in our family tree"?

DO: *action*. Where is it that God is asking you to shine brightly today? What help will you need?

SAY IT LIKE JESUS

CHAPTER 11

SAY IT AUDIBLY

Driving was one of Martin's spiritual gifts, or at least he thought so. He'd trained as a young driver to be as smooth as possible by balancing a cup of water on his dashboard and driving around the block as many times as it took until he hadn't spilled a drop. So when it came to becoming the primary driver for the work car-share scheme, the idea of looking after the environment, saving some money, getting to know some colleagues and exercising his driving gift sounded like a perfect match.

On his first pick-up of the day he ensured there was a vanilla skinny latte, extra hot, in the cup-holder waiting for Bob. And over the next few months he found all sorts of ways to serve and bless his fellow travellers. He kept waiting and praying for one of them to ask him why he went the extra mile.

But although the conversation ranged from football, to weather, to work gossip, nobody ever brought up the subject of faith. Perhaps his coffee kindness was enough.

Cold-callers, hard-sell marketeers, sales pitchers, courtesy callers, door-to-door salesmen. They all have their scripted and polished spiels and I am sick of them. They may be saying all the right words to get me to think about cheaper insurance, faster broadband, better service, but it just doesn't wash. I don't care what they are saying because I know they are just selling and don't really care about anything apart from meeting their own targets.

And so when it comes to talking to people about Jesus and about my faith, I know they will glaze over, bristle up or shut down, just as I do when someone is trying to sell me something I don't want or need.

Many Christians think that talking about faith implies a rehearsed, scripted hard sell that neither they nor their listeners can stomach, and so they end up not saying anything at all, in the hope that perhaps their lives will speak instead.

In a bid to justify this, a quote attributed to St Francis of Assisi has become one of the most popular sound-bites in the church. Strangely, the first Franciscan may never have actually said, "Preach the gospel, use words if necessary."[1] But in an age when many people are sick of empty words and broken promises, these words have a powerful resonance. Couldn't we just focus on being and doing like Jesus and miss out this whole section on saying it like Jesus?

If anyone could have communicated without using words, it was Jesus, Son of God and Saviour of the World. As the perfect image of the invisible God, Jesus lived out the character of God in the flesh. No one has ever been kinder, gentler, more compassionate or more gracious. But we cannot escape the fact that Jesus, the Word, modelled for us what and how to communicate with others. And his primary message was an invitation to believe the good news that the Kingdom of God was turning up.[2]

Jesus did not mime the gospel, he preached it. Not with a dog collar or microphone or clipboard. Not from a pulpit or from a script. Never with a fake smile and meaningless promises. His message varied radically, depending on where he was and who he was with, but the message was always unmissable, as Jesus would SAY IT AUDIBLY as well as visibly.

Jesus was more than a preacher. Everywhere he went, he healed and blessed and helped people. The gospels record that Jesus declared the good news both audibly and visibly, as good news and good deeds were always meant to go together. Peter summarized it like this in his address to the Gentile crowds:

> You know the message God sent to the people of Israel, announcing the good news of peace through Jesus Christ, who is Lord of all. You know what has happened throughout the province of Judea, beginning in Galilee after the baptism that John preached – how God anointed Jesus of Nazareth with the Holy Spirit and power, and how he went around doing good and healing all who were under the power of the devil, because God was with him.[3]

After this explanation of how Jesus preached and testified, he immediately goes on to show that, like Jesus, we too are to preach and testify, using words and deeds to help others know about the forgiveness available:

> We are witnesses of everything he did in the country of the Jews and in Jerusalem. They killed him by hanging him on a cross, but God raised him from the dead on the third day and caused him to be seen. He was not seen by all the people, but by witnesses whom God had already chosen – by us who ate and drank with him after he rose from the dead. He commanded us to preach to the people and to testify that he is the one whom God appointed as judge of the living and the dead. All the prophets testify about him that everyone who believes in him receives forgiveness of sins through his name.[4]

To be, say, do like Jesus, we should find ways to communicate his message with both words and deeds. We are not asked to make a choice between these two, as if they were somehow separable. Asking which of these is more important is like asking: Is it more important to love your mother or your father? Is it a higher priority to read your Bible or to pray?[5] Are your lungs or your heart more useful? What God has joined together in Jesus, let us not separate.

There is one exception. The same Peter who stressed in Acts that the message of words and the ministry of deeds were to go hand in hand, talks about one specific situation where words and actions are encouraged to be separated. This is in the pastoral context of Christian wives communicating the gospel to unbelieving husbands,[6] where continual evangelism would drive a husband away from both faith and family. Continual good deeds, on the other hand, could only serve the gospel's purposes. The New Testament scholar Ed Clowney puts it well:

> The silent eloquence of his wife's pure and reverent behaviour
> can preach daily the transforming power of Jesus Christ. No-one
> could be more emphatic than Peter has been about the place of the
> word of God in conversion.[7] Yet there are situations in which the
> silent witness of Christian love must support and prepare for the
> presentation of the truth.[8]

When Jesus and Peter called and invited and challenged people to turn to God, was it different to sharing our faith today? Were people more gullible in the first century? Were they more open to new ideas before the invention of planned sales presentation strategies? Were they less cynical before the modern-day scandals in politics and organized religion?

Actually, it seems that first-century Christians had more to lose than the average Western person living today. The noted evangelist Michael Green argues, "within thirty years of the founding of the new faith, to join the Christians meant to court martyrdom."[9] Despite this level of opposition, the first Christians were still bold and confident in asking people to respond to the good news about Jesus, a response that may have cost them their livelihoods, their families and even their lives.

Because of the stereotypes and preconceptions that surround the idea of "evangelism", the challenge to "Say it like Jesus" is, for most of us, a terrifying idea. But we shall see in the rest of this section that Jesus breaks all stereotypes. The way he speaks to people does not sound anything like a pre-recorded manipulative script trying to sell something. Whoever we are speaking to, we have a lot to learn from our Master about how to speak like him.

As Bob climbed into the car and asked, "How was your weekend?", a light went on in Martin's head. He began by raving about the football match on Saturday night, then explained how a couple of mates had ended up staying over, and then casually dropped in that he had gone to church on Sunday evening, where they had discussed faith and politics. He finished off by returning the compliment and asking Bob about his weekend. Would Bob celebrate with Martin about the final result in the match? Would he sympathize with him about having to conjure pillows from thin air for his unexpected guests? Would he question him about going to church? Or would he finally join the dots between Martin's careful driving and coffee provision and his Christian values and beliefs?

For further thought

BE: *reflection*. List your five biggest fears in evangelism.

Think of some occasions where it has been appropriate to talk about your faith outside of church. How did you feel? What were the responses?

SAY: *discussion*. List the reasons why we find it easier to share our faith visibly rather than audibly.

How much do you think Martin ought to talk about his faith in the car journeys? How would you bring up the subject if you were in a similar position?

DO: *action*. Pray for opportunities this week to drop in appropriate conversation starters about your faith. Aim to say something about your faith this week, however small and casual.

CHAPTER 12

SAY IT EMPATHETICALLY

Tuesday, 6 p.m.

Come on, come on! Chris jabbed impatiently at the "Close" button on the lift, but its doors were intransigent. Why was life always so hectic?

His friends at church seemed to think that as a single guy he had a lie in every morning, cruised through his day, and spent countless hours every evening playing *Call of Duty* on the Xbox 360. But they were wrong. His alarm was set for 6 a.m. and he left for work at 7. Twelve packed hours later, he would arrive home again with extra work to finish off, and the cooking, cleaning and washing to do. He was lucky if he got to the gym and his cell group once a week, although he never missed football training on Saturday mornings at 8 a.m.

Now his church had asked him to pray for five people and speak to five people about Jesus, and tonight he was supposed to report back. He had prayed for two, spoken to none and he had two hours left.

Just as the lift doors finally got the message, Tim from finance ran and squeezed through the closing gap. Chris saw his opportunity and launched in:

"I used to be scared of lifts – you know, too many horror stories – but since I became... err... a Christian, I'm not as frightened about death. Really... Do you ever think about...

you know... death, God, that sort of thing?" Chris let the question sink in, feeling quietly proud that he had the guts to bring up the subject, albeit awkwardly.

Tim glared at him. "You know my mother passed away last week. How dare you be so deliberately insensitive!" The door opened and Tim marched off.

Chris was left in the empty silence. He felt so ashamed. He couldn't face cell group now. Perhaps he would never share his faith again.

I can think of plenty of conversations I have started that have turned into verbal car crashes, scattering debris and victims. Many a time I have vowed never to even open my mouth again. Like the time when I was moaning about changing nappies, and didn't know that the girl I was talking to had just miscarried. Like the time I accepted an invitation to John's surprise party – except now it wasn't a surprise any more.

Jesus would have never made those mistakes. He was the sinless Son of God, the Saviour of the World, and he knew what was in people's minds and hearts and thoughts and histories. That had to be a huge advantage in any conversation. He knew exactly the right thing to say at the right time to the right people. He never got it wrong with his tone or his timing, his tough content or his comic touch. He was perfectly empathetic, not only recognizing the exact emotions of the people he spoke to, but understanding why they were feeling that way.

So when we are called to speak like Jesus, where can we start? However hard we try to SAY IT EMPATHETICALLY, will we always be fumbling in the dark? However hard we try to speak about Jesus, are we doomed always to struggle, because we can never really know where people are coming from?

Just because we can't cross the Channel by walking on water, does not mean we are unable to follow the command to walk in the footsteps of Jesus.[1] Similarly, just because we can't know how many husbands a perfect stranger has had, or speak with disarming prophetic accuracy into every encounter, does not mean that we are unable to learn from Jesus how to be empathetic in our conversations.

Let's take a look at these famous words Jesus spoke to his disciples:

Do not let your hearts be troubled. Trust in God; trust also in me. My Father's house has plenty of room; if that were not so, would I have told you that I am going there to prepare a place for you? And if I go and prepare a place for you, I will come back and take you to be with me that you also may be where I am. You know the way to the place where I am going.[2]

These are amazing words of comfort spoken to disciples who were indeed troubled in their hearts, and wondering where on earth they were going to end up, how they were going to get there, and whether they would ever see Jesus again.

But if we see the context of the reassurance Jesus gives here, we see that there is much more to these words of comfort than first meets the eye.

It was the eve of the most important and difficult mission that has ever been attempted in the history of humanity. This was more perilous than the D-Day landings; Jesus was more outnumbered than the 300 at Thermopylae; more rested on this one moment of history than on the assassination of Archduke Franz Ferdinand. The next day would see death defeated, the sins of the world atoned for, God made fully accessible to humankind, and forgiveness made freely available. Jesus' death on the cross was the hinge-point of history, yet mere hours before the ordeal began, he called his ragtag bunch of friends aside and made sure they were OK.

If Jesus was not all-knowing, we could have imagined that he was oblivious to his impending agony, death and separation from God. Perhaps that would help us to understand how he was able to focus on the needs of his disciples at such a crucial time.

But Jesus knew exactly what was going to happen to him. He was under incredible pressure and he felt the fear and dread and temptation to walk away. And still he made the choice to see life from the perspective of his disciples. He understood that the tempestuous events of that week were taking their toll on his friends. He knew that what was about to happen to him would destabilize his young followers. He spoke comfort to them, even though he was the one most in need of emotional support that night.

If anyone needed some me-time that night, it was Jesus, but he was spending the evening with his friends. He did not bump into them in a corridor or a lift to deliver the message. It was during the course of a meal that he got down to the nitty-gritty of what they were really feeling and told them things that they really needed to hear. This was not some grand gesture or last-minute effort. Jesus spent his life putting others first and putting himself in their shoes. We have seen it before, when he is desperate for a drink at a well, or in need of some timeout by a lake. Whether it is the presence of a single woman or a huge mob, he puts his own needs to one side. We see it again as Jesus hangs on the cross in physical torment, but making the effort to make sure his mother is cared for,[3] and encouraging the thief on the cross next to him[4] that paradise awaits him.

Putting ourselves in others' shoes and putting them first does not come naturally. For many of us, listening does not even come naturally, let alone speaking words of comfort, help, encouragement. These are things that we need to practise. Enjoying relaxed meals together with friends is a good place to start. Developing a habit of speaking empathetically is part of our challenge to live the Jesus way. Speaking empathetically as a habit will also help us when it comes to sharing our faith. Talking *with* people, not *at* them, will open natural opportunities to explain what we believe and why.

Chris stopped the lift on the next floor down and decided to walk back up a flight of stairs to the finance department.

He found Tim's cubicle and, fumbling for words, apologized. He asked if he could buy Tim a drink, as he knew something of the pain of losing a parent recently, and promised there would be no more God talk tonight. It was a shame to miss cell group, even though he would have had to admit his failings.

Tim, not really wanting to go back to an empty flat anyway, surprised himself by taking up Chris's offer.

For further thought

BE: *reflection*. If you were Chris, how would you play the conversation that evening over drinks? What would be the important things to say? What would be the best questions to ask?

SAY: *discussion*. Which of the following lessons from Jesus would help you to have meaningful heart-to-heart conversations?

1. Chatting over a meal.

2. Discussing the future.

3. Being open about spiritual things.

4. Talking about our feelings.

5. Sensitivity to the needs of others.

DO: *action*. Which of the following could you do this week?

6. Invite someone round for a meal.

7. Make time to listen to someone in need.

8. Forgo some "me-time" for the sake of somebody else.

CHAPTER 13

SAY IT HONESTLY

It had been a fairly innocuous question: "How is your family doing?" But twenty minutes later, tears were rolling down Tammy's face. She had started explaining how her daughter was struggling to find friends at university, and it had led to a whole story of regretted decisions the family had made over the previous eighteen years. They shouldn't have moved so often... They should have had another child... They shouldn't have forced her to persevere with the violin... They should have helped her become more independent... The phrase "If only we..." was a constant trope in the narrative.

Jenna had listened intently, asking questions often, offering nods and smiles and hugs in large measure. Eventually Tammy stopped. "I can't believe I have spoken for so long about me and my family! Thank you for listening. How are things with your Tom?"

The answer shot straight out of Jenna's mouth: "Oh, fine." She really wanted to leave it there. After all, Christians were supposed to be the ones who had it all together. But after Tammy had been so vulnerable, perhaps she should open up a little bit more than she was used to.

Did you know that smiling produces the same pleasure equivalence as 2,000 bars of chocolate? Did you know that children smile around 400 times a day, while most adults smile less than 20 times a day?[1] Did you know that Mother Teresa once said: "I will never understand all the good that a smile can accomplish"?

It seems that smiling is good for us, and good for others, but over time we adults seem to lose our ability to smile at the world. This used to worry me as a student, so I used to try to fall asleep with a smile on my face, in the hope it would become a permanent feature. Honestly! I felt like smiling was part of my Christian witness. I wanted to encourage my friends that God really did give joy, whatever difficulties I faced in life.

Sadly, I don't think I am alone in this naive view. Nothing can rival the ubiquity of the single word "fine" in our churches. "Fine" is the way we try to convince the world that we can manage. "Fine" is the way we prevent ourselves from having to dredge up and then manage our complicated emotions. "Fine" is the way we can fend off the majority of people from probing any deeper. "Fine" is the way we don't have to be a burden to anyone. Combine "fine" and a smile, and we have this Christian communication thing sorted.

But "fine" and a smile is not often the way we win others to Christ. "Fine" is not often the most honest response we can give. "Fine" is not usually the way we deepen our relationships with others. Guess how many people in the Bible say, "I'm fine." Nobody. "Fine" is not what Jesus would have said, even though he was the sinless Son of God, Saviour of the World, and knew that God had everything in hand. Rather than keeping a stiff upper lip, or internalizing his pain, or hiding his struggles, he is often recorded as expressing his sorrow, grief and longings.

We saw in the last study how Jesus did not allow his own distress to blind him to the needs and pain of others. But that same night, he also communicated his distress to the same group of friends. From Jesus we can learn what it means to truly SAY IT HONESTLY.

Then Jesus went with his disciples to a place called Gethsemane, and he said to them, "Sit here while I go over there and pray." He took Peter and the two sons of Zebedee along with him, and he began to be sorrowful and troubled. Then he said to them, "My soul is overwhelmed with sorrow to the point of death. Stay here and keep watch with me."

Going a little farther, he fell with his face to the ground and prayed, "My Father, if it is possible, may this cup be taken from me. Yet not as I will, but as you will."[2]

My attempts at a visage of immovable joy resembled a malfunctioning terminator robot, as my fixed grin was as false and as dubious as Arnold Schwarzenegger's acting. It did nothing for the salvation of my friends, let alone my much-needed student sleep. On the other hand, Jesus' ability to be honest about his suffering draws us closer to him as we see the full extent of his emotions and his authentic humanity.

Jesus knew the terrible suffering that sorrow and fear and dread bring with them. He also knew when and how to express those emotions appropriately, both to his disciples and to his Father in heaven. Jesus knew when he needed emotional support from others. Finally, he also knew that even when he was pushed to the limit, his Father's will was to be trusted.

Jesus was the Son of God, the Saviour of the World, and was perfectly emotionally balanced. We will naturally find it harder to express how we are feeling, but on the other hand, we won't have to bear the sins of the world in a cruel and torturous execution. Our deepest tragedies don't even come close to the suffering Jesus underwent that night.

In our attempt to say it honestly, sometimes we fall far short. We are bottled up so tightly that outwardly, we can appear to be emotionally as dry as a desert.[3] Some of us struggle to say anything at all about our emotions; we are always just "fine".[4] Indeed, Jonathan Edwards, the eminent American theologian of the eighteenth century, stated, "He that has doctrinal knowledge and speculation only, without affection, never is engaged in the business of religion."[5] Some of us have the opposite problem. Give us a chance to talk about our feelings, and we are like a burst fire hydrant, drowning anyone who listens to us as we pour out our soul.[6] Most of us tend towards one of these extremes. Jesus was neither a gusher nor a desert. He could both control and express his emotions. How can we keep these two things together as Jesus did?

Paul gives us a hint when reminiscing about his church-planting ministry in 1 Thessalonians 2:8. He writes: "Because we loved you so much, we were delighted to share with you not only the gospel of God but our lives as well." Sharing life with other people involves letting them in beyond the "fine" perimeter fence. It is here they will see what God is doing at the deepest and central parts of our character. Paul seems to have let both Christians and not-yet Christians inside his emotional defences. It is here we can give people a glimpse not of how great we are, but of how great God is. They get to see the treasure in jars of clay; they get to see God's ongoing workmanship in the reality of our lives.

In a time-starved culture, genuine conversation is a rare delicacy. The better we listen, the better chance there is for us to say something appropriate and helpful. The deeper we delve into other people's lives, the deeper they will understand our lives. Listening well and caring earns us the right to be heard.

This is not an instant-results mechanistic evangelistic technique. This is the way Jesus and Paul model to us a way of speaking the gospel into real lives.

When Jesus confided in his disciples, knowing that they were also emotionally exhausted and vulnerable, he also asked for their help. The vulnerability of Jesus helps us to relate to him. Jesus' openness makes him more of a Saviour, not less.

For some Christians, admitting need or vulnerability is seen as letting the side down, when actually it might be letting our defences down enough to let others in.

Jurgen Moltmann was an eighteen-year-old conscript into the German army in 1944, but by 1945 he was in a prisoner-of-war camp in Belgium, where he felt utterly God-forsaken. When someone gave him a copy of the Bible, the first copy he had ever read, he wrote:

> When I came to the story of the passion and read Jesus' death cry, "My God, why have you forsaken me," I knew with certainty, "This is the One who understands you." I began to understand the assailed Jesus because I felt that He understood me in my God-forsakenness; He is the divine Brother in distress, who takes the prisoners with Him on the way to resurrection and life. I began to summon up the courage to live again, seized by a great hope.[7]

This encounter so changed this young POW that he later became one of the twentieth century's leading theologians.

Sadly, when Jesus returned to his disciples a few moments later, he found them fast asleep.[8] He had let them see him at his lowest and they had let him down badly. Sometimes saying it honestly will not bring about emotional support, but added heartache. It is no wonder we protect ourselves with our "fines" and our smiles. Jesus knew that the disciples would let him down, but he was honest anyway. In the long run we have reaped the benefit from their failing. It is this Jesus who was both empathetic and honest, whatever the consequences, who we love and follow.

"It's kind of you to ask," said Jenna. "Actually, things aren't so fine at the moment. I have been struggling to know how to help Tom. He was bullied when he went up to secondary school and for a while he didn't want to go to school at all. We were really grateful for the help of a child psychologist in our church who pointed us in the right direction to get some help, but it's still hard for all of us."

Jenna's honesty with Tammy was a risk. Would she think less of her as her "together Christian friend"? Was she less of a support now she appeared so shaky herself?

Tammy's reply was, "Didn't prayer work, then?"

Jenna took a deep breath. She was going to have to dispel a myth or two about faith...

For further thought

BE: *reflection*. How can we be less "fine and smile" and more "open and honest"?

SAY: *discussion*. What issues do you tend to cover up as a Christian: marriage and parenting problems, theological doubts and questions, feelings of inadequacy and fears, personal ambitions and hopes, financial ups and downs, failures and embarrassments? Think of some ways to make these issues more approachable in your church.

DO: *action*. Think of three people you will see in the next couple of days that you know are wrestling with serious challenges at the moment. How can you be more approachable for them?

CHAPTER 14

SAY IT CREATIVELY

Ann was a born writer. She would find ideas in the queue at the supermarket as she overheard conversations. She would see people sitting at a train station and imagine their role in a tragic play. The news items conjured up in her head dramatic back-stories of violence and hardship. Ann would write these down either in her journal or in short stories she would sell every so often to magazines. She felt her life was caught up in narratives, tales and cameos. The troubled teenager from church she was mentoring felt the same way, and so Ann enjoyed helping her develop a novel in an attempt to make sense of her life's journey.

Ann's other evening out in the week was with her film group, and this week the movie had been traumatic and yet scintillating, raising all sorts of questions about life and death. After a few moments of silence, one of the girls just launched in:

"Ann, as the only Christian in the group, what did you make of that film?"

Ann, the born writer and great storyteller, suddenly found herself lost for words.

"First the worst, second the best, third the one…" "Jingle Bells, Batman smells, Robin…" "What do you get if you cross a kangaroo and a sheep?"

I have found it quite disconcerting to hear my small children coming home with chants, songs and jokes I used to know when I was their age, several decades ago, and a hundred miles away. My children haven't read them in a book. They are not spray-painted onto the tarmac outside classrooms. They are not part of the school's curriculum. They have just continued to circulate in the playgrounds virally, passed on from one child to another, crossing and surviving the generations. As my children get older, they are beginning to come home with fewer jokes and more strangely familiar urban legends. Again, these have wormed their way into their memories without revision or deliberate study.

Stories, it seems, have a life of their own. The American journalist Jane Didion put it poetically:

> We tell ourselves stories in order to live… We look for the sermon in the suicide, for the social or moral lesson in the murder of five. We interpret what we see, select the most workable of the multiple choices. We live entirely… by the imposition of a narrative line upon disparate images, by the ideas with which we have learned to freeze the shifting phantasmagoria which is our actual experience.[1]

One of the most powerful things about the way Jesus spoke was his use of stories. Saying it like Jesus must surely involve storytelling. But how can we possibly expect to tell stories like Jesus? He certainly has a head start on us: in Acts 2 Jesus is described as "the author of life".[2] Without Jesus, we would not have the grand narrative of the universe, a story in which Jesus is not only the author but the moral and the conclusion and the central character. He also happens to be the master of the parable, a storytelling genre that illustrates powerful truths in an unassuming and non-threatening format.

Although we cannot possibly match the creativity of the Creator God himself, he nevertheless has given us plenty of resources to SAY IT CREATIVELY.

Most of us don't realize it, but we are already pretty accomplished storytellers. A typical conversation will contain quite a few stories. We will talk about what we did the day before. We will have a moan about the saga with the new boiler and the leaking pipes. We will elaborate on the search for the lost keys. We will bring friends up to speed with a missed episode of our favourite soap. We will sympathize with a friend's parenting story by telling a few of our own. We will reminisce about the time when we missed the last train home, or got snowed in at work. We will muse about our own childhoods, or imagine outcomes to a current dilemma.

The stories may be told briefly or in great detail. They may be told with bitterness or with a sense of humour. They may be told sympathetically or manipulatively. They may be exaggerated or downplayed. However we tell them, it is these stories that make up a large proportion of our conversation, facilitate and deepen relationships, and also reveal who we really are and what we truly value.

Imagine your best friend begins a conversation by relating an incident with the supervisor or head teacher or chairman of the association that has obviously provoked great frustration and anger. Even without thinking, you will easily find yourself telling a story back – perhaps how the same person treated you in a similar way a couple of years back, or how you got the upper hand in a parallel situation. Your story communicates a level of sympathy with the friend's distress, but what has been expressed in terms of your gospel values or your attempt to follow Christ? What does an echoed story of character assassination and revenge actually reveal about you?

If I were to ask you to give a Christian response to the situation, you may suggest that you would encourage the friend to see things from another perspective, to ask for forgiveness, to make peace. But simply saying these things may give the impression we live on another planet, or are being critical, insensitive or holier-than-thou. Being creative like Jesus in the way we speak could imply a different tack. Maybe you could tell a story of an occasion when you misunderstood a situation, or remind the friend of an occasion where that supervisor did the right thing. By slightly tweaking our choice of stories, we can express something Christlike into a conversation. By being more creative, we can be instilling gospel truths into our relationships.

Creative storytelling is an important way Jesus chose to preach the gospel. Read the following extract from Mark's gospel:

Again he said, "What shall we say the kingdom of God is like, or what parable shall we use to describe it? It is like a mustard seed, which is the smallest of all seeds on earth. Yet when planted, it grows and becomes the largest of all garden plants, with such big branches that the birds can perch in its shade."

With many similar parables Jesus spoke the word to them, as much as they could understand. He did not say anything to them without using a parable. But when he was alone with his own disciples, he explained everything.[3]

We might imagine from many sermons that we have heard, that in order to explain to people what the Kingdom of God is, we need to prepare an essay. A lot of preachers base their sermon style on Paul's inspired letters, or John Stott's excellent commentaries, or notes from their Bible colleges. All of these are written forms of communication. But Jesus did not preach like this. The New Testament Scholar Tom Wright puts it well: "Throw a rule book at people's heads, or offer them a list of doctrines, and they can duck or avoid it… Tell them a story… and you invite them to share a worldview."[4] Jesus used parables and stories to invite his hearers to see what life in the Kingdom of God could look like.

The parables were not like fairy stories with a finger-pointing moral sting in the tail. They were more discreet, allowing the listener to be invited in, emotionally and imaginatively, but nevertheless containing gospel truth. Some of those truths were harder to work out than others. To the spiritually open, they tugged away at their consciousness like an unsolved crossword clue or maths problem. To the spiritually closed, the story was just a story.[5]

Although none of our stories will come with the same authority, creativity or insider information about the human psyche, there are three ways we can recreate Jesus' creative use of story in our own conversations.

First of all, as we saw earlier, we can choose our conversational stories with care, ensuring that the values are in line with the gospel. To the discerning, they will reveal a different way of viewing the world and beliefs about life, death and beyond.

Secondiy, we can tell our own stories. Human interest stories fill the pages of our magazines, soap operas and bookshelves – people will enjoy listening to us tell our own stories. Talking about Jesus' work in our life is also powerful, because no one can really argue with our personal history and experiences. Talking about the current work of Jesus in our life is also strong evidence that Christianity is not a dead faith but is continually relevant.

Thirdly, we can tell Jesus' stories. For example, we could use the parables themselves to illustrate a discussion about money, faith, relationships and so on.[6] Alternatively, we could tell the story of Jesus as narrated in the gospels. Becoming conversant with the plot line of the gospel and the little cameos of Jesus will not only help us to grow in our devotion and appreciation of Jesus; it will also help us to talk about him naturally and with confidence and creativity.

Ann poised herself on the edge of the leather seat in the coffee shop. She wanted to tell her friends how the film reminded her of the parable of the prodigal son, but wasn't quite sure how to go about it. Eventually she pulled out her smart phone and read from Luke 15, pausing every now and then to note the references the film had made to it and the way the director had deliberately come up with an alternative ending to it. As she ended she asked: "What do you think – did the director have this story in her mind when she made this film?"

For the next twenty minutes her friends discussed the film and the parable, happy to mull it over and relive their emotions before they parted company. For Ann, that parable had an extra significance. She hadn't shared about how this parable had helped her find faith many years before. Perhaps that would be a conversation for another time.

For further thought

BE: *reflection*. Reflect on conversations you have had in the past day or so. What stories have you told and what do they reveal about you?

SAY: *discussion*. Choose a television programme or film that has been popular recently. How could you chat about it in conversation in a creative way that promotes Christian values, or gets people thinking about spiritual issues?

DO: *action*. Pick one of Jesus' parables and reflect on it. In your conversations over the next day or so, see how many times you can allude to it directly or indirectly.

CHAPTER 15

SAY IT COMPASSIONATELY

"Did you see what she was wearing?"

"They say the boss is having an affair with her."

"With Shelley? Really?"

"Haven't you seen her in her low-cut tops and perfect fingernails, always stooping down to pick something up whenever he passes? Always the last one to leave the office in the evenings. Always waving the latest E. L. James novel around in her breaks."

"The suggestive little gold digger! That's one way to get ahead in this company."

"Especially when she can't keep track of the invoices."

"Clever, though. And who better to cover it up with a wife than a PA?"

"Look, she's coming in for her coffee break. Let's disappear."

"You coming, Ruth, or what? And why so quiet?"

We are experts at judging people. Thanks to *X Factor*, *Britain's Got Talent*, *Strictly Come Dancing*, *MasterChef*, *Dragons' Den* and many other popular television shows, we have been well trained to size people up by their posture, dress sense and looks, and that's even before they have got onto the stage. Is he a star in the making or another self-deluded wannabe? Does she get our vote, or our venom? We are encouraged to express our judgment on the phone, on social media, in the coffee lounge. We are encouraged to read everybody else's judgments in the papers and to hear their comments in the after-shows, by pressing the red button. It's compelling television, but is it reflecting a culture of judgmentalism or shaping it?

Jesus was not afraid to talk about judgment either. But he who made no bones about being the one to judge the living and the dead also had a lot to teach us about judgmentalism and how to SAY IT COMPASSIONATELY.

> *"Teacher, this woman was caught in the act of adultery. In the Law Moses commanded us to stone such women. Now what do you say?" They were using this question as a trap, in order to have a basis for accusing him.*
>
> *But Jesus bent down and started to write on the ground with his finger. When they kept on questioning him, he straightened up and said to them, "Let any one of you who is without sin be the first to throw a stone at her." Again he stooped down and wrote on the ground.*
>
> *At this, those who heard began to go away one at a time, the older ones first, until only Jesus was left, with the woman still standing there. Jesus straightened up and asked her, "Woman, where are they? Has no one condemned you?"*
>
> *"No one, sir," she said.*
>
> *"Then neither do I condemn you," Jesus declared. "Go now and leave your life of sin."*[1]

Somehow it was only the woman who was caught "in the act of adultery". The man's presence is treated as incidental, and he is somehow presumed innocent in the whole affair. The angry crowd scream for the law of Moses to be applied. The man's crime can be overlooked, but for the woman, no less than a public stoning to death will suffice. And to top it all, if they could just get Jesus to rubberstamp it, they could all join in the spectacle with a clear conscience. You can just imagine the crowd jostling to express their opinions, spread the gossip, and add their pebble's worth.

In the next chapter, Jesus will encourage a man treated unfairly by reassuring him that "For judgment I have come into this world",[2] but in this episode, with the teachers of the law and the Pharisees all waiting to hear him cast judgment in their favour, Jesus remains silent. Rather than condemn the woman who was caught red-handed, he gets his hands dirty by simply drawing a line in the sand and challenging the people in the crowd to judge themselves instead of judging the woman. One by one, they slowly slink away.

Judgment belongs to the sinless God and Saviour of the World, but here he refuses to pass judgment and sentence, and chooses to offer the victimized woman protection and forgiveness. Instead of baying for her blood, he is displaying grace for all to see. Does this mean that his standards for holiness and purity have slipped? Is he changing the rules? Is he okaying sex outside of marriage? Is he letting a first-time offender off with a warning? Not at all: as well as being willing to stand against the crowd, challenging them to judge themselves first, he is also willing to stand against the sin, challenging the woman to leave her life of sin. Grace and truth go hand in hand in ultimate compassion. Jesus is the last man standing when he lays down the challenge for sinless people to throw the first stone. He alone qualifies to cast judgment and rocks, but he chooses to do neither.

We may be living in a judgmental culture, but apparently Christians are seen to have crossed a line in this area. A survey conducted amongst 16–29 year-olds in the United States found that the top three words these young adults associated with Christians were homophobia (91 per cent), judgmentalism (87 per cent) and hypocrisy (85 per cent).[3] To counter these negative images of Christianity, it is even more important that we SAY IT COMPASSIONATELY like Jesus, who chose grace and refused to be judgmental.

Jesus has to stand against the crowd in order to stand up for a woman under threat of physical abuse, all the time knowing that the lawful consequence of her sin was indeed death. But he had come to offer another way forward. He could offer her forgiveness, knowing he would die in her place.

Living like Jesus often means standing against the crowd. Saying it like Jesus often means taking the side of the weak, the outcast and the downtrodden, no matter what they have done. Speaking up for those who cannot speak for themselves means getting our hands dirty through involvement in office politics, family politics, local politics and global politics.

Choosing not to be judgmental is a courageous step in today's society. It is not just choosing to keep our mouths closed when everybody else is casting rough opinions, it is choosing to speak compassionately to and about those who are being judged. Refusing to be homophobic, chauvinistic, critical, racist, and classist is one thing. Vociferously campaigning for the rights and dignity of those whom others condemn and persecute or overlook or take advantage of is another. It is perhaps here that we can make the biggest difference.

Dr Martin Luther King put this idea across well, saying:

We are called to play the good Samaritan on life's roadside... but one day we must come to see that the whole Jericho road must be transformed. So that men and women will not be constantly beaten and robbed. True compassion is more than flinging a coin to a beggar... We are called to be the good Samaritan, but after you lift so many people out of the ditch you start to ask, maybe the whole road to Jericho needs to be repaved.[4]

Ruth was torn. She couldn't condone an affair, but neither could she condone gossip. She didn't like Shelley particularly, and thought her flirtatiousness was out of order, but if she joined in the backchat, she knew she was no better. It was easiest to just keep silent, although that didn't help anybody.

A week later she spotted Shelley sobbing. Part of her was pleased – she had made her bed, and now she was lying in it. Then again, what would Jesus say? Back at her desk she sent Shelley a message: "Lunch?"

The reply was instant: "Lifesaver!"

For further thought

BE: *reflection*. What situations have you been in this week where you have been encouraged to be judgmental?

SAY: *discussion*. Do you think television shows are reflecting or shaping a culture of judgmentalism?

"If I tell someone off for being judgmental, aren't I being judgmental too?" How would you respond to this dilemma?

DO: *action*. Find some opportunities to counteract judgmentalism with grace this week.

CHAPTER 16

SAY IT HOPEFULLY

Monday, 8.15 p.m.

As Robert parked his car his stomach was telling him that he was looking forward to this monthly curry night, but the rest of him was less sure.

In theory he enjoyed hearing about everyone's news and stuffing limitless amounts of tasty food into himself while sitar music played on an endless loop in the background. But in practice there was a ritual, which began the moment the menu was handed out, and ended when they stumbled out the door. As the blokes outbid one another on who was going to have the hottest curry, Robert knew he would get the usual flack. They always laughed as he ordered the Korma they had nicknamed "Bert's dessert".

Shortly after the joking and the traditional news catch-up over poppadums, the conversation quickly descended into ever-more disparaging banter over the guys' girlfriends, bosses and cars. By the end of the evening, Robert knew that he would leave vowing not to eat or drink for several days, and also feeling slightly smug that whatever he was struggling with, someone else in the group was having a tougher time.

I am a hopeless extrovert. And one of the symptoms of this malaise for me is that I have a tendency to speak before I think. And so I greet the woman waiting in the ultrasound department and smilingly ask her when her baby is due. "I have kidney stones," comes the curt response. I welcome the man pushing the buggy into church by complimenting his daughter's beautiful curly hair. "That's my son Charlie," he replies. I am taking questions at the end of a sermon and point to the gentleman in the yellow sweater. "Actually, I am a lady and I was going to thank you – but now I'm not." As I turn fifty shades of red again, I often wish I could rewind and erase the last thing I said.

Words are powerful things. It only takes four words to get married: "I will" and "I do". The difference of one word can determine whether you are declared "Guilty" or "Not guilty" in a court of law. Even the mere tone of the word "Sorry" can make or break a relationship. Proverbs puts it like this: "The tongue has the power of life and death."[1]

I can think of lots of occasions where one or two words spoken out of turn or out of anger have caused me terrible heartache. I can also think of a few occasions where one or two carefully chosen, precious words have brought me immense comfort and blessing. A card before an exam or a difficult journey. A text as I wait for an interview. A kind greeting at a funeral. A note after a prayer meeting. Proverbs says about such messages of hope: "Gracious words are a honeycomb, sweet to the soul and healing to the bones."[2]

Jesus was the expert at using powerful, well-placed words to bring comfort, healing and hope. Zacchaeus was blown away when Jesus invited himself for tea. Mary was immediately comforted in her terrible grief when Jesus just uttered one word – her name. Two words, "*Talitha koum*", and a little girl was raised from the dead.

I wish my words could have this effect on people, instead of alienating and offending them, as is more often the case. But Jesus was the sinless Son of God and the Saviour of the World, and I am not. So what hope is there for me when it comes to me being able to SAY IT HOPEFULLY? Let's look at the following example to see what we can learn from Jesus:

> There was a written notice above him, which read: THIS IS THE KING OF THE JEWS.
>
> One of the criminals who hung there hurled insults at him: "Aren't you the Messiah? Save yourself and us!"
>
> But the other criminal rebuked him. "Don't you fear God," he said, "since you are under the same sentence? We are punished justly, for we are getting what our deeds deserve. But this man has done nothing wrong."
>
> Then he said, "Jesus, remember me when you come into your kingdom."
>
> Jesus answered him, "Truly I tell you, today you will be with me in paradise."[3]

The contrast here is striking. On the one hand, words of abuse both in the form of a written notice, nailed as an accusation above Jesus' head on the cross, and also in the form of mockery from a criminal being executed at the same time. On the other hand, words of comfort, spoken by an innocent victim, dying for the sins of the world.

In between is a simple request revealing that the convicted felon next to Jesus realized his own guilt, believed that Jesus was exactly who he said he was, and knew he needed mercy.[4]

Jesus needn't have responded. There he was, dying for the sins of the world. Suffering the excruciating[5] pain of the nails and the torture and the breathing and the humiliation and the abandonment by his Father. He was about to have his legs broken and take his final breaths. But even in the middle of this most important mission, Jesus makes the time and takes the effort to offer hope and help to the man dying next to him.

There is no lecture in store for a man who has lived a life of crime. There is no ten-week course for him to be enrolled on to. No prayer for him to repeat. No list of dos and don'ts. No doctrinal statements or membership documents to sign. Just a few encouraging words of comfort and assurance and hope.

For those of us who are scared of words such as evangelism and discipleship, Jesus' words are of great comfort to us too. A little hope can go a long way.

Tell a preacher he's good at telling stories and he will do it again. Tell a teenager you like the way they have done their hair and you will watch them grow an inch taller in an instant. Tell a young mum that she's doing a great job with her troublesome two-year-old and she will beam. Ask an elderly person how they are doing, and it may be the highlight of their week.

When I was at university there was a girl in my halls of residence from a Mormon family, who I used to love catching out. Whenever I caught her humming a Christmas song, I would jump in with a "Ha! I thought you Mormons didn't believe in Christmas." Whenever I discovered her making coffee for a friend in the kitchen, I would enjoy pointing out: "Ooh, evil Mormon coffee."[6] What an idiot I was. I could have encouraged her to sing the rich theology of the carols, or commended her for making a hot drink for a friend, even though she couldn't drink it herself. There were opportunities to spread hope but I just spread misery. I could have affirmed the ways that God was working in her life[7] rather than neutralizing them.

Choosing to offer words of hope, that are deliberately selected because they will build people up rather than tear people down, might not come naturally to us. I know that the more tired I am, the easier I find it to be cynical. The more stressed I am, the easier I find it to lapse into sarcasm. The busier I am, the more likely I am to use sharp or thoughtless words. Saying it, hopefully, like Jesus means catching ourselves and editing our language, tone and humour. It means choosing our words carefully to build people up.

As Robert parked his car his stomach was telling him that he was looking forward to this monthly curry night, but the rest of him was less sure. Yes, he was worried about the banter. No, he didn't like being on the receiving end of the jokes, and no, he wasn't very good at dishing it out or batting it back either.

Tonight, he decided nervously, he was going to spice things up. It wasn't much, but hopefully it would be a step in a different direction. In his backpack he had printed off a pub-style quiz, and he was determined to end the evening by praising one or two of his mates for their pop knowledge or mental maths.

Unfortunately, he could only think of one way to signal this shift in tone and curry (!) some favour with his friends: he was going to have to order the Tikka…

For further thought

BE: *reflection*. Think of a time when someone spoke "gracious words" to you that were "a honeycomb, sweet to the soul and healing to the bones." What was it about those words that made them sweet and healing?

SAY: *discussion*. Why do you think we often find it easier to remember harsh words spoken against us rather than hopeful words spoken to encourage us?

Look over Luke 23:39–43. What advice would you give to someone who had a natural tendency to always see the negatives or had a propensity to complain and grumble?

DO: *action*. Edit your language, tone and humour today to add an element of hope into every conversation.

CHAPTER 17

SAY IT ABSOLUTELY

Tuesday, 4.59 p.m.

It had been a long day, and everyone had worked hard.
People had volunteered their time and energy to sit in front of
cameras and lights and tell emotional stories of what God was
doing in their family lives. Take one. Take two. Take seventeen.
Sit here. Smile here. Answer this question. Answer that
question. By the end of the afternoon their patience was still
holding out, just about, although when pizza was mentioned,
there was a hint of a sparkle in their eyes.

It wasn't until a week later that Emma found out they had
paid double. Chris had paid by credit card over the phone at
the point of order, and then David had paid the delivery guy in
cash.

When Emma phoned for an apology, the staff flatly denied
the error, and refused to offer a refund. But Emma was not
going to let them get away with this – she had a plan.

"Resentment is like a glass of poison that a man drinks; then
he sits down and waits for his enemy to die." The man who
spoke these words had made the hard decision not to allow
the venom of resentment to slowly destroy him. Nelson
Mandela was imprisoned for twenty-seven years for fighting
for freedom, and spent eighteen of those years on Robben

Island enduring long days of hard labour. But when he was eventually freed he spoke not of revenge and retribution but of forgiveness and absolution.

I am shamed by stories like this because I find it hard to forgive those who cause me even minor hassles in my day. I am still angry with Royal Mail for losing a parcel months ago, and I still tense up when I remember that time when I was met with bureaucratic baloney after a local train station had only given me half of the return ticket I had paid for.

Everyone knows that forgiveness is an essential part of the Christian life, a powerful healer and an effective witness, but few of us know how to do it.

Forgiveness is tough. It contradicts most of our instincts. When someone causes us pain, everything in us screams to either hurt them back or to run far, far away. It is hard to treat the perpetrator as though it had never happened. It is hard to live without recalling those painful memories. It is hard to keep bitterness and resentment at bay so they do not poison our dealings with others. It is hard not to put the record straight, not to see justice done, not to have our pain acknowledged, not to hear an apology.

Alexander Pope's words are often quoted: "To err is human, but to forgive is divine." Jesus, Son of God and Saviour of the World, was in a unique position to offer forgiveness. His death ultimately ensured that the injustices and injuries of the world would be dealt with once and for all. But perhaps Pope was wrong. Forgiveness is not only for Jesus; it is for us too. Jesus commanded that we should forgive,[1] and in the heart of the Lord's Prayer is the implication that we put that command into practice: "And forgive us our debts, as we also have forgiven our debtors."[2] But how can we possibly learn to absolve people from the way they have hurt us and forgive absolutely like Jesus did? How can we SAY IT ABSOLUTELY? We need to orient ourselves around that pivotal moment when humanity's greatest error met the Divine's most powerful act of forgiveness.

As the soldiers led him away, they seized Simon from Cyrene, who was on his way in from the country, and put the cross on him and made him carry it behind Jesus. A large number of people followed him, including women who mourned and wailed for him. Jesus turned and said to them, "Daughters of Jerusalem, do not weep for me; weep for yourselves and for your children. For the time will come when you will say, 'Blessed are the childless women, the wombs that never bore and the breasts that never nursed!' Then 'they will say to the mountains, "Fall on us!" and to the hills, "Cover us!"' For if people do these things when the tree is green, what will happen when it is dry?"

Two other men, both criminals, were also led out with him to be executed. When they came to the place called the Skull, they crucified him there, along with the criminals – one on his right, the other on his left. Jesus said, "Father, forgive them, for they do not know what they are doing." And they divided up his clothes by casting lots.[3]

In the middle of the chaos, the wailing of those who mourned the dead man walking, the mockery of those who bayed for his blood, the brutality of the soldiers and the agony of crucifixion, Jesus performs a miracle. In the middle of the savagery, he prays. He does not call down curses on those who are mercilessly torturing him. He does not command a million angels to his aid. He offers forgiveness.

Some say he was offering forgiveness to the soldiers who were just following orders. Some say he was offering amnesty to the religious leaders who were so blinded by tradition that they couldn't see God was in front of them. Some say he was offering pardon to the crowds who mocked and taunted him. Whoever the prayer of forgiveness was meant for, the act of Jesus' sacrifice meant forgiveness was ultimately available for all. Forgiveness was offered to all of us who have ever ignored God, spoken an angry word, thought a malicious thought, conspired against another person, gone with the crowd, or failed to love our neighbours as ourselves.

Jesus is the only one qualified to forgive absolutely. Only Jesus was the Lamb of God who took away the sin of the world.[4] Only Jesus has the authority to forgive sins, and the ability to remove our sin from us as far as the east is from the west.[5] And it is only because of Jesus that we too are able to forgive.

Jesus has not only opened the way for true and absolute forgiveness through his death on the cross, he has also modelled to us how that forgiveness should be offered.

First, forgiving others is intrinsically linked with our own forgiveness by God. Jesus is clear in the Sermon on the Mount and the Sermon on the Plain and in several of the parables that the two must go together.[6] We forgive as we have been forgiven.[7]

Secondly, forgiveness is not about feelings. As he hangs on a cross suffering the effects of their brutality, Jesus chooses to extend forgiveness. Some say time is a healer, and that it is easier to forgive, the longer we wait, and there may be some truth in that. But Jesus does not wait until they express their remorse or beg for a fresh start; he models the choice to forgive in the middle of his excruciating pain.

Thirdly, forgiveness is costly. If someone does something unquestionably wrong against us, it feels natural to seek justice and vengeance. To forgive is to choose not to exert that right. Forgiveness accepts not only that we have been wronged, but also that we will get no compensation. By taking this double hit, we pay disproportionately, in order that the perpetrator can go free. This is what saying it absolutely is about. Absolving someone from the pain they have caused offers absolute freedom and absolute forgiveness.

When we understand that this is the costly forgiveness we have received from God, we begin to realize that this is the forgiveness we have to extend to others. God allows us to experience absolute forgiveness, and he equips us to offer absolute forgiveness. Pope was right – the forgiveness we offer is divinely sourced.

Thomas Merton, the twentieth-century mystic, wrote:

We do not really know how to forgive until we know what it is to be forgiven. Therefore we should be glad that we can be forgiven by our brothers. It is our forgiveness of one another that makes the love of Jesus manifest in our lives, for in forgiving we act towards one another as he acted towards us.[8]

Emma had several ploys at the ready. She could refuse ever to order pizza from this company again. Or she could order a pizza from them and refuse to pay them. She could name and shame the company on Twitter. She could start a social media campaign demanding a refund. She could write to the head of the company, explaining her frustrations. She could ask her solicitor to threaten the company. She could actually go to the small claims court. She could write to the newspaper. She could stalk and harangue the delivery guy who refused to give her a receipt.

But as a Christian she struggled. Which of these options were legitimate ways of reaching an agreement, and at what point should she cut her losses and offer forgiveness?

For further thought

BE: *reflection*. Read and reflect on the following prayer by Nikolai Velimorovic, a Serbian bishop who spoke out against Nazism in the Second World War and ended up in a concentration camp in Dachau. There, reflecting on his betrayal not by atheists, nor by the Nazis, but by his fellow believing clergy, he wrote these powerful words:

Bless my enemies, O Lord. Even I bless them and do not curse them. Enemies have driven me into your embrace more than friends have. Friends have bound me to earth; enemies have loosed me from earth... Enemies have made me a stranger in worldly realms and an extraneous inhabitant of the world.

Just as a hunted animal finds safer shelter than an unhunted animal does, so have I, persecuted by enemies, found the safest sanctuary, having ensconced myself beneath Your tabernacle, where neither friends nor enemies can slay my soul.

Bless my enemies, O Lord...[9]

SAY: *discussion*. Have you ever been in a situation like Emma's? How far should she go to get recompense? At what point does practising forgiveness at this micro-level enable us to forgive at a deeper level?

DO: *action*. Spend some time reflecting on the forgiveness God has offered you.

CHAPTER 18

SAY IT CRITICALLY

Jen was in a bad mood. Her housemates were playing music far too loudly for her to be able to concentrate on her seminar paper. She had also received a letter from her phone company charging her extra for data usage that should have been free with her package, and now she had just found out that the operation her mum had been waiting months for had been delayed.

If only she could get this paper finished, then she could make some phone calls to get to the bottom of the other two problems. But she just couldn't concentrate. Any second now and someone was going to get the full force of her pent-up fury – probably the annoying, insensitive neighbour singing along to Justin Bieber at full volume.

I caught myself apologizing the other day. That wouldn't necessarily have been a bad thing, except I was apologizing to the electronic self-checkout machine at my local supermarket. No, I hadn't used any of my own bags. And before I even realized, I had said "Sorry" out loud.

According to the anthropologist Kate Fox in her book *Watching the English*,[1] it is not my fault. It is down to my British heritage that I have an "apology reflex". She conducted an experiment on the London Underground, deliberately bumping into people, and found that we are more likely to apologize than not, even when it's not our fault. Since reading her book I keep catching myself apologizing – for turning up five minutes early for a dentist appointment, for the lack of parking in my cul-de-sac, and even for the weather at our neighbourhood barbecue.

This tendency to say sorry can have an effect on how we speak to others about our faith. For some of us, even mentioning the name of Jesus can cause us to backtrack quickly with some form of apology. If we are not careful we can end up with a doormat-discipleship, where we Christians overplay gentleness and meekness, and lose our call to be a prophetic challenge.

In our often mawkish, mewling, whimpering excuse for Christianity, we end up giving the impression that Jesus is more like a pet kitten than the Lion of Judah, as Revelation describes him.[2] The Jesus revealed in the New Testament is gentle Jesus, meek and wild. He is both compassionate and passionate.

There are times when Jesus speaks harshly and critically. Usually it is to the Pharisees and teachers of the law. Occasionally it is to his own disciples. When does saying it like Jesus mean we need to get tough and speak out, challenging with hard truths clearly and strongly? Or are we exempt from this because we are not the Son of God and Saviour of the World?

> *"Woe to you Pharisees, because you give God a tenth of your mint, rue and all other kinds of garden herbs, but you neglect justice and the love of God. You should have practised the latter without leaving the former undone.*
>
> *"Woe to you Pharisees, because you love the most important seats in the synagogues and respectful greetings in the marketplaces.*

> "Woe to you, because you are like unmarked graves, which
> people walk over without knowing it."
> One of the experts in the law answered him, "Teacher, when
> you say these things, you insult us also."
> Jesus replied, "And you experts in the law, woe to you, because
> you load people down with burdens they can hardly carry, and you
> yourselves will not lift one finger to help them.
> "Woe to you, because you build tombs for the prophets, and
> it was your ancestors who killed them. So you testify that you
> approve of what your ancestors did; they killed the prophets, and
> you build their tombs...
> "Woe to you experts in the law, because you have taken away
> the key to knowledge. You yourselves have not entered, and you
> have hindered those who were entering."[3]

The most compassionate person in history does not mince
his words here. He is not backward in coming forward. He is
relentless in his critique, shocking his listeners. Those that are
used to judging the holiness of others have their credentials
ripped from them. Jesus judges the judgmental. He criticizes
the critical. He cuts through the pretence of the pretentious,
exposing their superficial spirituality, their double standards
and their hypocritical attitudes. The religious leaders were
happy to receive honour and dish out shame, but Jesus
honours the shamed with grace and shames the honourable
pious. Jesus is incensed by the fact that those who were
supposed to be leading God's people were failing so miserably
to show his grace and compassion. He is outraged that their
profession of faith is all show and no substance, all rules and
no righteousness, all judgmentalism and no justice.

But surely we can't emulate Jesus' blistering critique? Surely
none of us has the right, the authority or the information to
speak so directly to another in the same way? None of us are
without sin, so surely none of us can dare to throw stones?

We are told to speak the truth to one another in love.[4] And
Jesus is an example to us in word and deed. There will be

times when we need to SAY IT CRITICALLY like Jesus, as we challenge both Christians and non-Christians. So how and when should we do this?

First, we are to speak up for others. Jesus did not defend himself: when they hurled insults at him, he did not reply.[5] But he did speak strong words on behalf of others. Jesus is critical of the Jewish leaders of his day because their example and their influence was corrupting others and making God's love less accessible to the people who needed it most.[6] Our critical words cannot be unleashed because of a personal slight or a bruised ego. Jesus teaches us to hold back and only use our harsh words from a genuine desire to help others.

Secondly, we are to speak out with love.[7] Jesus' anger is not the explosion of a hothead; there is no red mist, no malice in his motives. Jesus' anger is driven by his love. Jesus does not criticize in order to humiliate or character assassinate the leaders. His harsh words are like a slap in the face to a hysterical person. He speaks harshly to rouse his adversaries out of their self-deluded spiritual stupor. When sweet words are too easily dismissed, strong words are needed to communicate the importance and urgency of our message. But our strength must be motivated and tempered by our love for those we seek to engage with. The American Christian poet and author Wendell Berry puts it well: "The Christian gospel is a summons to peace, calling for justice beyond anger, mercy beyond justice and love beyond forgiveness."[8] When we are called to love our enemies, sometimes that means we love them enough to challenge them.

Thirdly, we are to speak out with the truth. Jesus spoke with surgical precision. Rather than writing off everything about the religious leaders, he systematically and specifically exposed their delusions, even though they would continue to ignore him. When we are prompted to criticize or challenge, we must be careful not to exaggerate and not to escalate, instead speaking only the truth clearly and boldly.

Saying it like Jesus means not only knowing what to say, but when to say it, who to say it to, and having the courage to not hold back. It means knowing when to speak tender words of comfort and tough words of challenge. We are not the Son of God, Saviour of the World, and sometimes we will get it wrong. That is the time we need to turn on our apology reflex again for real and say a sincere "Sorry".

Jen was bottled up so tight, she felt like she was going to explode. She took a deep breath. She needed to let off steam but she didn't want to boil over and leave a trail of singed relationships in her wake. She scribbled down all the things that she was upset about, and listed how she could respond instead of react. As she looked at her list she decided it was right for her to champion her mum's cause. It was the third time they had rescheduled. So she picked up the phone, took another deep breath and asked to speak to whoever managed Dr Archer's diary. "I'm sorry," she began, "but..."

For further thought

BE: *reflection*. What does it mean for the church to speak the truth in love not only to one another but also to those in authority? Do you think your political engagement has involved too much love or too much criticism?

SAY: *discussion*. Have you ever been in a situation similar to Jen's? What happened next? Think of some situations where it is right to offer forgiveness, and others where it is right to offer criticism.

DO: *action*. There are lots of situations around the world where Christians need to speak words of comfort and words of challenge. Use your online voice to do this today.

CHAPTER 19

SAY IT CONFIDENTLY

Thursday, 9 a.m.

Dr Peters was nervous. She believed in bringing her faith to work, but this morning she had heard from a colleague in another local authority who had invited a child patient to his church holiday club and was now being accused of abusing his power and trying to brainwash children. She was praying that none of her patients would be the kind of people that needed prayer today. She was going to keep things nice and professional and formal.

This was a secular country and she had a secular job. Her husband, a web designer working for a fizzy drinks company, never hid Bible passages on the site, and her best friend, a graphic designer, never deliberately left little pictures of crosses in the shadows of the photos she was editing. So why should Dr Peters be worried that she wasn't bringing her faith to work?

"Mr Singh?" she asked inquiringly in the waiting room, trying not to catch the eye of the man in the turban, just in case she was accused of racist stereotyping...

In October 2012 a fourteen-year-old hit the headlines. Malala Yousufzai had written for the BBC, explaining what life was like under Taliban rule. She knew the danger she was putting herself in and talked about it often. Nevertheless she fearlessly campaigned for the rights of girls to receive an education. Because of this, the Taliban attempted to assassinate her, shooting her in the head.

In June 1989 a lone student wearing a white shirt and a black pair of trousers took a stand against the Chinese military while the world watched on in awe and horror. He single-handedly stood in the path of the armoured tanks rolling into Tiananmen Square, pausing them temporarily before they used live fire to silence the demonstrators who were calling for government accountability.

These stories of immense courage from people who claim no Christian faith force me to consider whether my beliefs have any substance, and challenge me to ask how far I am willing to go to speak out for them. The challenges I face as a Christian in the UK seem pretty light compared to the persecution these two young people faced.[1] Yet many of us struggle to be open about our faith, for fear of the repercussions. The freedoms we enjoy are so much stronger than those either in the Swat region of Pakistan or the streets of Beijing, and yet we are often afraid to show even a fraction of the confidence shown by these two young revolutionaries.

Whether Jesus was speaking to the wind and waves, or the sceptical religious leaders, or demons, or dead and diseased bodies, he always demonstrated a clear authority in the face of opposition. In order to learn to what extent we can SAY IT CONFIDENTLY like Jesus, perhaps the best place to look is how he spoke when he was at his most vulnerable:

> But Pilate answered, "You take him and crucify him. As for me, I find no basis for a charge against him."
> The Jews insisted, "We have a law, and according to that law he must die, because he claimed to be the Son of God."
> When Pilate heard this, he was even more afraid, and he went back inside the palace. "Where do you come from?" he asked Jesus, but Jesus gave him no answer. "Do you refuse to speak to me?"

Pilate said. "Don't you realize I have power either to free you or to crucify you?"

Jesus answered, "You would have no power over me if it were not given to you from above. Therefore the one who handed me over to you is guilty of a greater sin."

From then on, Pilate tried to set Jesus free, but the Jews kept shouting, "If you let this man go, you are no friend of Caesar. Anyone who claims to be a king opposes Caesar."[2]

To anyone watching, the contrast couldn't have been starker. One man dressed in fine clothes, believing he had the authority to condemn and the power to crush. One man dressed in rags, beaten and scourged and silent, his bleeding body bearing witness to the cruelty and barbarism directed against him. But Pilate, the Roman governor of the region, nevertheless felt threatened by Jesus, and tried to assert his authority by reminding Jesus just who was in control.

Faced with the might of the Roman Empire, Jesus spoke confidently. He didn't flinch or back down or cave in under the pressure. He responded to Pilate by steadily reminding him of the sovereignty of God in the situation. This response was enough to frighten an already uneasy Pilate.[3]

Jesus had every right to be confident. He had a different perspective. The ruler-versus-criminal scenario was entirely reversed. This was not a question of whether the ruler, Pilate, would find Jesus guilty, but of whether the sovereign God would hold Pilate guilty. And so, even as he experienced the pain and anticipated his death, Jesus was unafraid to put the governor in his place.

Jesus had no lawyers, no demands, no militia, no band of supporters at his side and no online petitions. He made no attempt to impose his power or evade his death. Yet from his position of weakness, he confidently undermined Pilate's authority by reminding him who was really in charge.

Not that long afterwards, we read of a few similar situations where the powers that be were threatening some uneducated upstarts and getting more than they bargained for. Instead of scaring them, as they intended, they found themselves in shock. The reaction of these religious bullies to the disciples' confidence was recorded for posterity: "When they saw the courage of Peter and John and realized that they were unschooled, ordinary men, they were astonished and they took note that these men had been with Jesus."[4]

We may not be the Son of God and the Saviour of the World, but when we spend time in his company, his character, courage and confidence should rub off on us, just as it did for his first disciples. We may never face being sentenced to death, but sometimes we will need to stand up and stand out, speak up and speak out for Jesus. To do this, we are clearly shown in Scripture a perspective in which it is God who holds supreme power, and we are given a confidence that comes from the Holy Spirit who lives in us.[5]

According to the World Evangelical Alliance, over 200 million Christians in at least 60 countries are denied fundamental human rights solely because of their faith. In the UK we are very unlikely to be persecuted for our faith to this degree, but many of us feel marginalized, threatened, disrespected, belittled, sidelined and ignored. A change of perspective, so that we remember God's sovereignty,[6] and a challenge to speak confidently will not necessarily end our own suffering in the situation; in fact, they may intensify it.[7] Nevertheless, this is the way that Jesus models for us, and he calls us to speak for him.

To speak confidently, we need to look to God, the true authority in the universe, and we need to look to our brothers and sisters in places like Sudan and Pakistan, who are courageously speaking up for Jesus, even though they could lose their jobs, their homes and their lives. Strangely, we may even need to look at the courage of people who do not know Jesus, to be inspired to be confident in our sinless Saviour.

Mr Singh and his turban sat in her office and Dr Peters used all her professional skills to diagnose his ailments and refer him for some further tests. She felt called to be a good doctor to everyone, whatever their beliefs or backgrounds, and she enjoyed helping people find wholeness and comfort.

She noticed that as he left he glanced over at a framed picture on her wall. It was a decorated verse from the Bible that her children had made for her birthday. When she had put it up she had prayed that it would be a comfort not only to her, but perhaps also to her patients. "God is our refuge and our strength, an ever present help in times of trouble," said the picture.

Dr Peters felt even more nervous now – would Mr Singh report her for crossing a line? Or would those words speak to him? Should she take the picture down, or keep it up?

For further thought

BE: *reflection*. Reflect on the following verses:

When you are brought before synagogues, rulers and authorities, do not worry about how you will defend yourselves or what you will say, for the Holy Spirit will teach you at that time what you should say.[8]

There is an assumption here that we will be put in situations where we will need to defend our faith, and that we will feel out of our depth. Where does this happen for you?

SAY: *discussion*. What would your advice be to Dr Peters? How do we live wisely yet confidently in our post-Christian context?

DO: *action*. How can you stay in touch with the needs of brothers and sisters facing persecution around the world? You might want to subscribe to prayer updates from organizations like Open Doors, Release International or Christian Solidarity Worldwide.

CHAPTER 20

SAY IT SILENTLY

Juela's bus ride was always interesting, as thirty schoolchildren regularly caught the same bus with her, announcing the latest gossip down the aisles, complaining about the trials of homework, and laughing at snapshots posted on Facebook.

You could tell which day of the week it was just by the volume. Fridays were the noisiest by far, and Juela found the language that she heard from eleven-year-olds shocking: it was definitely post-nine o'clock watershed vocabulary. The F-word was used as a punctuation mark, people's mothers were insulted, even racist and homophobic phrases were bandied around without objection.

But what really made Juela's skin crawl was the casual use of her Lord's name. "OMG" was the loudest blasphemy of choice, and day after day Juela wondered what impact it would have if she literally stood up for what she believed and told them she found their swearing offensive. Would she shock them into respect? Or would she become a laughing stock, unable to face boarding the 340 to Edgware again?

Silence is a rare commodity. It is hard to get away from the sounds of music, traffic, workmen and advertising slogans constantly bombarding our eardrums. Even at night the rain, the cats, the car engines, the "pings" of emails on my mobile phone provide a dissonant backing track for my slumber. It is no wonder I often sleep through my alarm clock.

Silence is also a powerful means of communication.[1] Deliberately giving someone the silent treatment, for example, can be excruciatingly frustrating for them. When I was a student I used to hitch a lift to university with a housemate. When she was upset she wouldn't utter a word for the entire journey, and with a glare she demanded the same of me. Those twenty minutes were a painfully long time for an extrovert – I used to wish she would just shout at me!

Alternatively, some people resort to silence out of fear. One friend says that when her husband walked out on her and her three children, he simultaneously and inadvertently alienated her from most of her friends. People who used to chat to her on the street now avoid her. She believes people are silent because they are afraid of saying the wrong thing, even though there is no right thing to say that will magically put her life back together again. To her, their silence communicates not only a lack of sympathy, but an indifference to her pain that betrays how little they value her friendship.

We began this "Say It Like Jesus" section with a challenge to be audible about what we believe and why, because nobody can guess the gospel from the silent witness of deeds. But there were times when Jesus was silent. Was he doing it to deliberately annoy or was he genuinely afraid? Or was there good reason? When do we say it best when we SAY IT SILENTLY? Let's take a closer look at Jesus' silence in his trial, and see what we can learn:

When Herod saw Jesus, he was greatly pleased, because for a long time he had been wanting to see him. From what he had heard about him, he hoped to see him perform a sign of some sort. He plied him with many questions, but Jesus gave him no answer.

The chief priests and the teachers of the law were standing there, vehemently accusing him. Then Herod and his soldiers ridiculed and mocked him. Dressing him in an elegant robe, they sent him back to Pilate. That day Herod and Pilate became friends – before this they had been enemies.[2]

The silence of Jesus is not to be overlooked in this passage. It was not out of fear or exhaustion. It was neither accidental or coincidental. This dramatic silence was prophesied 700 years earlier in Isaiah 53, a passage that speaks of Jesus' death in amazing detail: "as a sheep before its shearers is silent, so he did not open his mouth."[3]

Herod, at the beginning of this passage, is quite pleased with himself. He has the latest trend in entertainment within arm's reach, and is happily anticipating a front-row view of the infamous miracle-worker in action. But Jesus has nothing to say to Herod. It is a dangerous place to be in when God has given up speaking to you.

Herod had been given lots of chances to hear and respond to God. He had heard God speaking through John the Baptist when he was under his lock and key. But eventually he could stand it no longer. Herod had jumped at the chance to silence John's critique of his marriage to his sister-in-law, beheading him at the request of his wife and daughter. So Jesus refuses to answer Herod's demands or his questions. His silence communicates a judgment on Herod.

My natural tendency with my non-Christian friends is to try silence first – perhaps they will ask me about the books on my shelf, or the sticker on my car, or my opinions on life, the universe and everything. When they don't, that's when I try a more audible approach to sharing my faith. But perhaps we have got this the wrong way round. Perhaps it is just fear that makes me lead with silence. Jesus was silent only when the opportunity to receive the message of good news had been rejected.

Included in the Sermon on the Mount is an awkward instruction to us disciples of Jesus: "Do not give dogs what is sacred; do not throw your pearls to pigs. If you do, they may trample them under their feet, and then turn and tear you to pieces."[4]

This verse is not instructions on providing a good diet to our pets or our livestock: no Jewish person would ever have dreamed of keeping pigs. Instead, this is advice on how and when to speak.[5] It is part of a passage that talks about being discerning and not being judgmental.[6]

Jesus was not silent out of fear or out of spite. He knew that an on-demand miracle would have no effect.[7] He was silent because he knew words were no longer needed.

We are often silent about our faith because of fear or spite. We have already been challenged in this book to speak out in compassion and in confidence. However, there is a place for a discerning silence. When words are inappropriate; when words are unacceptable; when words are insufficient, then sometimes our profound silence speaks volumes.

Juela asked herself a few questions: Will challenging thirty teenagers on a bus on a Friday night about their language have the desired effect of eliminating blasphemy? Will it promote the gospel? Will it build bridges between Christians and unchurched young people?

She decided to stay silent. She got off the bus a stop early and purchased a pair of headphones before walking the rest of the way home. As the bus overtook her, she wondered if there was anything she could do to help the next generation to discover the greatness of God and to learn to respect the Christians in their community.

For further thought

BE: *reflection*. Today, make space and time in your day to be silent for five minutes. Don't read or write. Try to be on your own. Use the time to reflect and listen to God. How comfortable do you find it? What can you learn from silence?

SAY: *discussion*. What would you advise Juela to do about the situation on her bus home?

Reflect on the strange words of Jesus, "Do not throw your pearls to pigs." Does this advice apply to any situation you are facing?

When is it right to be audible about your faith, and when is it right to be silent?

DO: *action*. Where are the opportunities for you to speak up for your faith today? Where are the situations where you have said enough, and now silence, prayer and a good visible witness are the best ways forward?

DO IT LIKE JESUS

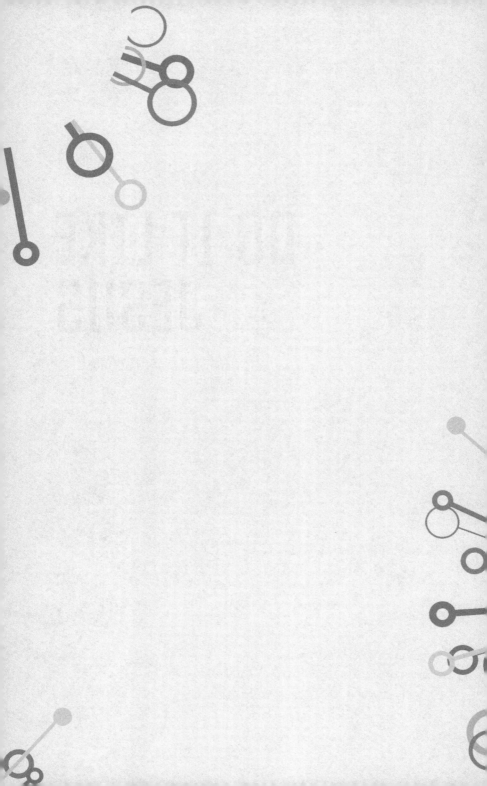

CHAPTER 21

DO SMALL

Monday, 11.20 p.m.

The big day was approaching. He had invited everyone he could think of, but surprisingly, only about half of his friends were able to come and even less of his wider family.

Bob began to consider who the reliable people in his life were. How many friends did he really have? How many were merely colleagues and acquaintances?

But something more troubling was gnawing at his mind. This was a big milestone birthday, one of those with a big zero at the end. He had always thought that he would have done something significant by now. The big job had never really come up. The big break had never really happened.

With this birthday, no matter how he looked at it, he was definitely in the second half of his life. Was it going to be the beginning of his grand finale or the end of his big flop?

Size matters. Our culture says that we need to live it large, maxing out our credit cards while minimizing our carbon footprint.[1] Our portions get super-sized but our waistlines need to be tiny. Our televisions get bigger and brighter and our phones get smaller and smarter. Size matters at church too. Leaders often give the impression they want bigger churches, fuller meetings, deeper commitment and larger offerings.

Bigger is supposed to be better, and so when we think about the impact we are making on the world, we can easily get discouraged. When we look at Jesus, our impact on the world is microscopic in comparison to his. It is good to be thinking about how we can influence the world for the Kingdom, but following Jesus might mean living smaller rather than bigger.

If Jesus had wanted international fame, he should have been born into a Roman ruling dynasty, but instead he chose to be born into a destitute Jewish peasant family. If Jesus had wanted to build a platform for a big ministry, then he should have headed for Jerusalem on day one, but instead he "wasted" most of his ministry on the small towns and backwaters of Israel. If Jesus had wanted to gather a power base, he should have spent more time with the big-shot religious elites and less time with sinful small fry. He should have made a big deal over the dinner invites he received from the rich and famous. He should have lapped up their compliments rather than belittling their religious showmanship. He shouldn't have been so large hearted to the least and the last if he wanted to make it big in the world.

Why did Jesus deliberately choose to DO SMALL? In the following passage he gives us a clue:

> *Then people brought little children to Jesus for him to place his hands on them and pray for them. But the disciples them.*
> *Jesus said, "Let the little children come to me, and do not hinder them, for the kingdom of heaven belongs to such as these."*
> *When he had placed his hands on them, he went on from there.*[2]

Jesus' disciples get lots of the menial jobs – feeding the crowds, booking the upper room, being watchmen in the Garden of Gethsemane. Here we see them doing some security, time-management and day-care duties, as they try to protect Jesus by vetting those that are allowed to see him. They believe that the big man has no time for little people. But Jesus tells the disciples they have made a huge mistake this time. He rebukes them for discounting the significance of the children and argues that infants are the model for those who will receive the Kingdom of God.

What does Jesus mean by this? How are children to model entry to the Kingdom of God? Do we all need to be short and gullible and have milk teeth? The answer is provided just a chapter previously, when Jesus calls a child to be his visual aid, saying, "whoever takes a humble place – becoming like this child – is the greatest in the kingdom of heaven."[3]

Jesus himself models this childlike humility as he breaks with the convention of his day, which gave very little time for children, let alone rights or privileges in society. He calls us to have the humility to do the small things that are necessary to honour God rather than the big things necessary to impress other people.

For Jesus, it's not the big show of public devotion that counts, it's the quiet prayers in a small private room that matter.[4] For Jesus, it's not the large donation with the public fanfare that counts,[5] it's the invisible widow with her infinitely small offering.[6] For Jesus, it's not about the impressive religious elites, it's about the young impressionable children. Jesus takes pleasure in and makes time for the small.

This is a difficult message for some of us. We feel that the quick wins, the big impact, the large numbers automatically imply success. But what if we allowed God's priorities to challenge the ones we have picked up from our culture? What if, instead of trying to please the millions, we tried to please the one and only true God?

Who would have thought a baby born in a forgotten backwater of the Roman Empire would be the Son of God and the Saviour of the World? Who would have thought that a man dying a criminal's death on a Roman cross on a dark day outside the city limits would be the most powerful act of love this universe would ever witness? Who would have thought that a homeless person[7] hanging out with the kids would teach the world a great lesson in humility? In God's economy, bigger isn't always better; sometimes it's the small acts that matter most.

Jesus searches out those hidden from the spotlight – Zacchaeus up a tree, the blind, the lepers, the children. The fact that Jesus enjoyed the company of the apparently insignificant is encouraging news for most of us. First, because we can be confident he enjoys spending time with us. Secondly, because if we checked through the call history on our phones, or the appointments in our diaries, we probably would not find a list of A-list celebrities, but names unknown to the world at large. The time we spend visiting an elderly relative, the small acts of kindness to a neighbour, the way we invest in the children in our church community, the text message to see if someone is OK, the cards we write to offer condolences or congratulations: none of this is ever going to make headline news but all of it matters to God.

In our celebrity culture, where the lives of the rich and famous are continually in the headlines, it can be easy to think of the good we could do if only we had more time or money. Instead, today our challenge is to DO SMALL like Jesus – looking for the seemingly insignificant tasks that can actually be accomplished well for God.

Bob knew that no journalist would ever write a biography about his life. He was not going to be voted Sports Personality of the Year. And nobody would ever make an action figure modelled on his physique. There were no Nobel Prizes he was in line for.

Twelve people came to his big birthday bash out of the fifty or so he had invited, but they had a fantastic evening. He got some great gifts too, but his favourite was the card he received from Anton, hand drawn, but unmistakably a picture of his nephew riding his bike with a big smile on his face. Bob remembered that day well. They'd gone up and down that street so many times, he still remembered where the potholes were. He was glad it had taken all day, because every hour they were out was an hour his sister got to herself, and she had really needed it that weekend.

As he pinned the card up on his wall, Bob realized that it was in this small relationship that he could make the biggest difference.

For further thought

BE: *reflection*. Napoleon Hill, author and adviser to President Franklin Roosevelt, said, "If you can't do great things, do small things in a great way." Mother Teresa said, "We can do no great things; only small things with great love."

To what extent do achievable, small things in our lives get pushed to the side, because we are too busy pursuing the big things that are beyond our reach?

SAY: *discussion*. What are the "small" things in our lives that we can do for God?

How can shifting our focus onto the small things affect both the way we view others, and the way we view ourselves?

What would it mean for your church to DO SMALL?

DO: *action*. Make a list of small things you could do this week. For example: send an encouraging text. Chat to a child at church. Read one chapter of the Bible. Lend one book. Check that the receptionist at work is feeling well. Go running with a friend. Consider keeping a log to watch how this makes a difference in your own life or in the lives of others.

CHAPTER 22

DO WORK

Tuesday, 7.30 p.m.

It was prayer meeting time again. To be honest, it wasn't the highlight of Steph's month. It was another night out, or worse still, another night in. After putting the kids to bed she had a nine-minute window to clear up toys, apple cores, shoes, bike helmets and stuff a packet of biscuits onto a plate before the doorbell began ringing.

Predictable as ever, Su and Bob arrived first. They both spoke at once, jumping from one topic to another without pausing. In between some allotment anecdotes, holiday plans and grandchildren stories, Steph thought she detected some friction. Even after she had moved into the kitchen she could hear Su complaining loudly about how over-committed they were and how little time they had to themselves.

Before she knew it, Steph had stormed in: "Please stop moaning. I haven't had an unbroken night's sleep in four years. I always eat my dinner standing up while I try to juggle feeding the baby and serving the rest of the family. I am on six different church rotas, and haven't heard a sermon in over a month because I have been called back into crèche with a child who won't be left. I would love to have time to even dream about growing my own carrots and sightseeing in Turkey – so please don't moan about not having enough time under my roof."

It came out a lot louder and sharper than she expected, so
she hastily retreated back to the kitchen to try to locate some
clean mugs and calm down before everyone else turned up.

I admit it. I am a serial eavesdropper. I can't help listening in
to conversations around me on the bus, on the train and in
the coffee shop. Most of them begin quite predictably as the
people complain, or possibly brag, about how busy they are.
The teenagers have too much homework, the students have too
many deadlines, the graduates are buckling under pressures
of work, the unemployed have countless applications to write
and assessments to complete, the parents are running around
after their children, and even the retirees seem to be living
life in the fast lane. All of them are struggling to find time to
do the things they really want to do, and most of them are
struggling to fit in even the basics of family time, leisure time,
and church time.

In a society that has virtually cured or eliminated the age-
old affliction of boredom, we all have to manage the levels of
busyness we experience and our expectations of work and
leisure. Sometimes we need to be challenged by the realities,
restrictions and responsibilities of life and the call of God on
our time. The average person[1] works fewer hours than our
forebears, and has over five hours of leisure time a day, but
somehow we feel like we have more work and less rest.[2] We
desperately need to work out our rhythms.

It has been said that Jesus came "to disturb the comfortable
and comfort the disturbed",[3] but sadly, often when we
communicate about work, we comfort the comfortable and
further disturb the disturbed. It is especially important over
these next two chapters that we listen carefully to what God is
saying to us in these challenging areas of work and rest.

First of all, is it even possible that we can learn about work
from Jesus? Certainly, he had a very clear job to do on earth,
but his job description was unique to him as the Son of God
and Saviour of the World. Jesus never had to sit in an office,

work a forklift truck, take minutes in meetings, complete risk assessments, do stock inventories, give a multimedia presentation or report back to a supervisor. So what does the Bible say about how we DO WORK like Jesus? In the following passage we see how Jesus challenges the accepted rhythms of work:

> Meanwhile his disciples urged him, "Rabbi, eat something."
>
> But he said to them, "I have food to eat that you know nothing about."
>
> Then his disciples said to each other, "Could someone have brought him food?"
>
> "My food," said Jesus, "is to do the will of him who sent me and to finish his work. Don't you have a saying, 'It's still four months until harvest'? I tell you, open your eyes and look at the fields! They are ripe for harvest. Even now those who reap draw their wages, even now they harvest the crop for eternal life, so that the sower and the reaper may be glad together. Thus the saying 'One sows and another reaps' is true. I sent you to reap what you have not worked for. Others have done the hard work, and you have reaped the benefits of their labour."[4]

At first sight, Jesus' words are rather alarming. He and his disciples have just walked many miles uphill in a hot climate, but while Jesus sits down by a well for a rest and a drink, the disciples continue their journey in the midday heat, to get some provisions for lunch. When they get back they find him in conversation with an outcast woman with a troubled relational history, after which he seems to refuse the food they have just gone out of their way to acquire.

Jesus is not being rude. John places three similar narratives back to back to point to a significant lesson that he is trying to teach us about Jesus. First of all, Jesus talks to Nicodemus about being "born again", but Nicodemus understands it literally as a physical rebirth. Then Jesus talks to the woman at the well about "living water", which she thinks is an actual physical drink. Now here, Jesus talks to his disciples about food, but they assume he is refusing the physical food they have in front of them.

Jesus is not denying the physical needs to be born, to drink and to eat,[5] but he uses these essential human processes as metaphors for our spiritual needs. We need to enter the Kingdom of God, we need to constantly be refreshed by his Spirit, and we need to constantly be nourished by cooperating in his work.

Jesus does not see his work as a necessary evil, a means to pay the bills, a temporary burden or a commitment he would rather do without.[6] No, he sees work as an extension of his relationship with the Father. His attitude to work is that it is as satisfying as a good meal, as fulfilling as bringing in the harvest and as refreshing as polishing off some fresh bread in the middle of a long journey.

If only the work we do was energizing instead of exhausting, was inspiring instead of irritating, was driving our worship of God instead of distracting us from our worship.

Jesus' view of work as ultimately satisfying was God's original intention for us. Humans were made to work in cooperation with and obedience to God. The word "vocation" is derived from a Latin root that means "voice" or "calling". Os Guinness explains: "Calling is the truth that God calls us to himself so decisively that everything we are, everything we do, and everything we have is invested with a special devotion, dynamism, and direction lived out as a response to his summons."[7] Ideally, we will have this sense of call not just about the paid work that we do, but about all the other areas of responsibility we take on, as everything that we are involved in has the potential for being an opportunity for worship.[8] Whether we work in the financial sector, healthcare, town planning, arts, social work, education, international diplomacy, retail or technology, or whether we are running our local tennis club, cooking meals for our family, gardening, writing, caring for elderly relatives or driving – anything that we consider work or responsibility can be nourishing for us and others in our relationship with God.

Jesus knew that living in a fallen world, the human experiences of toil and thirst and hunger and tiredness are real. He experienced all them. However, because we often get overwhelmed by our earthly appetites and perspectives, Jesus reminds us over and over again of God's take on these things.

Jesus' calling led him into great pain, frustration[9] and sacrifice, and we should not be under any illusion that our work, careers or vocations will mean that we experience a continual warm glow of satisfaction through every aspect of our working life. Every job, every role will include boring, unfulfilling, even agonizing elements. But if we can never see past that to the ultimate goal of seeing God's Kingdom built, or if we never experience a sense of fulfilment, then perhaps this is an indicator that we are giving our time to the wrong things.

Jesus at work showed us these moments of incredible delight and moments of incredible distress. As we are not the Son of God, Saviour of the World, we do not expect to experience anything like the extremes that Jesus did. However, for most of us, our work oscillates between some levels of fulfilment and frustration. Jesus challenges us to search out and feed on those satisfying times, allowing them to nourish our soul, drive our worship of God, and help to see us through the difficult times.

As the kettle boiled in the kitchen, Steph cooled down. She had said more than she had meant to, but she had meant most of what she had said. She could hear Bob and Su sitting in unnatural silence in the lounge.

She reluctantly made up the tray of refreshments and went back to apologize, knowing exactly what they would say – a profuse offer of help, a heartfelt regret, wishing they could relive those precious parenting moments when their own children were small, an apology for being insensitive.

As Steph waved the last people out of the door that night, she found to her surprise that her kitchen had been left spotless. She went upstairs to kiss her beautiful sleeping children goodnight and flushed with pride, knowing that no travel experience or bunch of vegetables would ever come close to the wonder of parenting these little bundles of joy.

As she turned off her bedside light, she heard the first scream of the nightshift...

For further thought

BE: *reflection*. Read Luke 10:38–42. How do we know when our work or our responsibilities are turning into an idol?

SAY: *discussion*. What advice would you give to Steph, who seems to be getting no time to herself as a young mum? When was the last time you complained/bragged about being too busy? How do we decide where to draw the line between being busy and too busy?

DO: *action*. Say grace, as you do before a meal, before you begin each task today, to remind you that work is a gift from God to nourish your soul and help others.

CHAPTER 23

DO NOTHING

Wednesday, 10 a.m.

Wednesday was the worst day of the week for Billy. The weekend feel-good factor had well and truly worn off sometime on Tuesday afternoon, and by Thursday the next weekend was beginning to come into view. But there was nothing good about Wednesdays. It was the dark day with no light at either end of the tunnel. There were no incentives on Wednesdays to help him get out of bed in the morning. Not even a riveting TV show scheduled for the evening to keep him going through the day. Thank goodness today his brother in Sweden had messaged, offering him an online gaming appointment at 9 p.m. That would just give him time to squeeze in a couple of soaps and a chat to his girlfriend before he could leave that Wednesday hinterland behind him for another week.

Watching my son eat roast dinner is one of those time-warp moments. He eats the vegetables first, clearing them off the plate as quickly as he can in reverse rainbow order, closely followed by the roast potatoes and Yorkshire puddings, so he can slow down and savour the most important part of the meal that he has saved until last – the meat.[1] It is my weekly déjà-vu moment – this is exactly what I did as a thirteen-year-old too!

It occurs to me that this strategizing of a meal is not only a video replay of a mini-me, but also a parable of the way many of us approach our working day. Some of us have parts of our day we don't like – chores, commuting, work responsibilities – and we rush through it as quickly as possible in order to get to the meat of the day – leisure, family and rest. On the other hand, some of us endure the mundane parts of our life (e.g. cooking, family, cleaning and sleep) so we can sink our teeth into our work – the most satisfying and nourishing part of our day.

In one sense, at least, we are all having a rhythm of work and rest, so what's the problem? At least my son is eating his vegetables, right? Actually, we may find we need to check for balance not only in terms of time, but also in terms of attitude. Work and leisure are two of the biggest idols in our society today. If we are either working so we can live, or living so we can work, we are in danger of demoting the rightful place of God in our lives.

We have already seen how Jesus models for us how to do work. Now let's see what Jesus has to say about how to incorporate rest into our lives; or in other words, how to DO NOTHING.

Mark's gospel is a busy gospel.[2] It is told in terse language, and we see Jesus rushing around from one place to the next. Yet at least seven times in Mark's short gospel we see Jesus making space for solitude, prioritizing personal prayer and taking time out for rest and restoration. Let's take a closer look at one of these occasions:

> *Then, because so many people were coming and going that they did not even have a chance to eat, he said to them, "Come with me by yourselves to a quiet place and get some rest."*
>
> *So they went away by themselves in a boat to a solitary place. But many who saw them leaving recognized them and ran on foot from all the towns and got there ahead of them. When Jesus landed*

and saw a large crowd, he had compassion on them, because they were like sheep without a shepherd. So he began teaching them many things.[3]

This passage hints a little at the pressure Jesus and the disciples were under. Life was so busy that they didn't always have time to eat, as the crowds were always demanding more from him. Here we see a brief interlude of rest between two very intense ministry sessions, and it teaches us some important lessons.

First, rest did not just happen naturally. Some of us have to actually put time off into our diaries, or it would not happen at all. If the Son of God needed to make time for rest, how much more should we?

Secondly, Jesus did not tell his disciples to just brave it out or carry on regardless. Without any show or big speeches, he just slips away to try to get the rest that is long overdue.

Thirdly, Jesus takes his disciples with him. He not only makes sure he is getting a break, but that those around him are getting a break too. For those of us who have leadership roles, this is an important principle. Do we enable others to take not only appropriate amounts of time off, but also effective time off?

Fourthly, Jesus includes his disciples. Sometimes Jesus needed time on his own, sometimes a retreat with his disciples was good enough down time. For those of us involved in busy family life or living in a community, time off with people around us doesn't always feel like a rest! There are bikes to fix and problems to solve and meals to make and conversations to initiate and board games to win. We may need to adapt our expectations. For Jesus, time off did not exclude those closest to him. Being in their company was a form of relaxation.

Fifthly, Jesus' time off was not sacrosanct. Shortly after they reached their solitary place, they were spotted, and the crowds and work returned in force. For some of us, taking a few days' break from work means coming back to overflowing inboxes, backlogs of marking, and misunderstandings to correct, and we wonder whether it was all worth it as we come back to work with a bump. Jesus knew that his rest would be cut short, but he still prioritized his time out. Whether it is the delivery man ringing the doorbell at 7 a.m. on our lie-in day, or our holidays getting interrupted by a family crisis, compassion should still win out.

Finally, Jesus worked so that we could rest. In Matthew's gospel he makes us a direct invitation: "Come to me, all you who are weary and burdened, and I will give you rest. Take my yoke upon you and learn from me, for I am gentle and humble in heart, and you will find rest for your souls. For my yoke is easy and my burden is light."[4]

Jesus' invitation is not to a new religion, a new structure, a new fad, a new project, a new job or a new institution. He invites us to come to him to get the rest we all need. We may have wonderful holiday experiences, but at the end of the day, only Jesus can set us fully at rest. But strangely, Jesus combines this offer of rest with the offer of a yoke. A yoke is not a good symbol for rest. Surely a pillow, a sun lounger, or a massage would have been much more suitable. Yokes make us think of work – those wooden collars for cattle working a plough, or worse, for slaves doing forced hard labour. But in the first century yokes may have been used to symbolize something different. Michael Green argues: "Metaphorically, the yoke was used to describe the law which the Jewish youth undertook to bind to himself in the bar mitzvah ceremony. It spoke of loyal commitment."[5] In other words, our rest comes from living in allegiance to Jesus. It is through walking in the footsteps of Jesus, and putting him first in our lives that we learn to manage the rhythm of work and time off, and find the ultimate rest.

As my son wolfs down his vegetables, I hope that one day he'll learn to enjoy combining the flavours and textures rather than mentally grading each part of the meal separately. Perhaps we too can learn to integrate rest and work better in our everyday life, developing a healthier pace of life that allows us to follow Jesus more closely and more sustainably.

As Billy caught himself zipping through work, he felt like he was driving at 50 mph through a 20 mph zone outside a school. If he carried on going this fast, he might get to where he wanted to be more quickly, but potentially he could cause a lot of damage on the way.

He knew his work and not just his leisure mattered to God and therefore should matter to him, but he just couldn't feel it. Did he need a new job? Would it be better when he got the promotion? Or did he need a new approach to his work?

He decided to experiment with consciously slowing down, looking for things to enjoy, being attentive to others, treating his job like it actually mattered to him. Hopefully he could keep it up beyond next Tuesday.

For further thought

BE: *reflection*. Reflect on Jesus' words:

> Come to me. Get away with me and you'll recover your life.
> I'll show you how to take a real rest. Walk with me and work
> with me – watch how I do it. Learn the unforced rhythms of
> grace.[6]

SAY: *discussion*. How would you advise Billy? At what point should he consider looking for a new job?

How do you balance those rhythms of work and rest, as discussed in the previous two chapters? What are your most effective means of time off or time out? How can you make sure you fit those into your day/week/year?

DO: *action*. Check your heart – are you living for rest, work or Jesus? Check your diary – have you made plans for rest in your life? Check your friends – how would they describe your work/rest rhythm?

CHAPTER 24

DO SOMETHING

"Child slavery is the biggest problem facing the global church today."

"Hunger kills more people than AIDS, malaria and tuberculosis combined."

"Nearly 10 million children under five die each year: most of these deaths are preventable."

"One billion people – that's one seventh of humanity – go to bed hungry."

"Every twenty-two minutes a child is taken into care in the UK."

"More than half a million women die in pregnancy and childbirth each year."

Rosie felt if she heard another appeal for her money or time, she would explode. There were so many needs and so many worthy causes – how could she possibly make a difference? Which crisis should she focus on? How much money should she give?

She asked for advice via her Facebook page, and got an array of responses. Some of her friends encouraged her to champion particular issues they felt passionate about. Another friend wrote that it wasn't worth the effort trying to fix the unfixable problems in the world – she should just focus on local evangelism instead. A relative told her that as long as she was concerned about these issues, she was on the right path.

But none of these responses seemed to help her. What should she do with the little she could offer?

The sheer scale of the needs in the world today often paralyses us because it looks like we can't actually make a difference. Is this sense of powerlessness one of the reasons why we find it relatively easy to allow ourselves to find distraction? Do the countless ways of entertainment mean we are less likely to worry about the global challenges? Do we spend more time planning our holidays than fixing our priorities? Do we spend more time thinking about our next phone deal than about the next five years of our lives?

As Christians, we know the danger that too much entertainment and consumption effectively distracts us not only from the raw realities of our world and our neighbours, but also from listening to God's voice and following in the footsteps of Jesus. But Jesus was not powerless in the face of world issues. As the Son of God he demonstrated that he had unlimited power over disease, hunger, and even death. So why, then, did he not eliminate the killer diseases of his day and at least pause the problems of hunger, child abuse, slavery and maternal mortality? When he could so easily have done everything, he only did something. For us, who could so easily do nothing, what does it mean to DO SOMETHING like Jesus?

Jesus went through all the towns and villages, teaching in their synagogues, proclaiming the good news of the kingdom and healing every disease and sickness. When he saw the crowds, he had compassion on them, because they were harassed and helpless, like sheep without a shepherd. Then he said to his disciples, "The harvest is plentiful but the workers are few. Ask the Lord of the harvest, therefore, to send out workers into his harvest field."[1]

All of Jesus' healings were, in one sense, temporary. Everybody that Jesus healed got terminally ill in the end. Even the people he raised from the dead passed away again eventually. So why did Jesus do so many healings? And should we pay more attention to them? Lesslie Newbigin, the great missionary theologian, wrote:

Jesus habitually healed sick people... One fifth of all the material in the four gospels is concerned with the healing of physical diseases. The virtual ignoring of this by most of Christian history is one of the astonishing facts which the theologian and historian must try and explain.[2]

Many Christians believe that a person's spiritual well-being is far more important than a person's physical well-being and that therefore it is right to focus on Jesus' teaching ministry and ignore the many gospel accounts of Jesus' healing ministry. But Jesus seemed to make no such distinction.[3] In the passage above, his teaching, evangelism and healing ministries are interwoven, demonstrating a holistic or integral approach to mission.[4] His compassion for the crowds includes their practical and spiritual concerns and led to both practical and spiritual help.

Fighting disease is always a losing battle, even for the Son of God. And medics today will attest to this in their experience: despite all their successes and medical breakthroughs, eventually everybody they help will one day succumb to cancer or heart disease or some other killer. Yet Jesus did not see his work as futile. Jesus bothered. He chose to DO SOMETHING rather than nothing.

The healings of Jesus are a taste of the future.[5] They are a trailer for the time when there will be "no more death or mourning or crying or pain".[6] They are an invitation to faith and hope – the vital means by which we become citizens of the coming Kingdom.

Only God can bring his Kingdom, but we are called to be part of God's taster campaign. We will never alleviate all poverty or eliminate hunger or find a cure for death, but that is not our job. Our task is to bring a small taste of faith and hope into these situations so that we point people towards the ultimate Saviour of the World.

The kind word we speak to a neighbour, the care we take of our local town, the money we give to help a water project, the fair-trade purchase we make is our bit-part in the trailer for God's coming Kingdom, spreading reasons for people to hope in God.

Everywhere Jesus went he started rumours and sowed seeds of hope and demonstrated in relatively small ways that God's Kingdom was coming. And he taught his disciples that part of our job of following him and loving him is doing the same, and that if we do not, we are in big trouble:

> Then he will say to those on his left, "Depart from me, you who are cursed, into the eternal fire prepared for the devil and his angels. For I was hungry and you gave me nothing to eat, I was thirsty and you gave me nothing to drink, I was a stranger and you did not invite me in, I needed clothes and you did not clothe me, I was sick and in prison and you did not look after me."
>
> They also will answer, "Lord, when did we see you hungry or thirsty or a stranger or needing clothes or sick or in prison, and did not help you?"
>
> He will reply, "Truly I tell you, whatever you did not do for one of the least of these, you did not do for me."[7]

These are possibly the most harrowing words in the Bible. Not just because Jesus mentions eternal fire and the devil, but because we see here that indifference and lack of compassion are seen as satanic and punishable with the same ferocity as the enemies of God. This is an even more sobering passage because Jesus is not talking to serial killers, war criminals and rapists about punishment, but to ordinary upstanding members of society, people who were sure they were right with God. None of them had robbed a bank or abused a child or assassinated a president – but they similarly faced God's wrath because of what they had neglected to do. They had not even offered a simple drink to their thirsty neighbour, or a blanket to a homeless person, or a listening ear to a prisoner. Jesus so identifies with the suffering, the destitute and the outcast that he feels their lack of compassion as though he were on the receiving end.

The New York-based Bible teacher Tim Keller provides another angle on this passage:

On the Judgment Day, don't say to the Lord, "When did we see you thirsty, naked and captive?" Because the answer is – on the cross! There we see how far God was willing to go to identify with the oppressed of the world.[8]

The crucifixion is Jesus' ultimate act of identifying with the vulnerable and the needy. If Jesus was willing to identify that closely with the poor, no wonder he asks us to be wiling to do something to help meet the physical and emotional needs of the poor in our communities.

Jesus' words are not arguing that we are forgiven by God as a reward for doing good deeds, acts of compassion or works of justice. Rather, our relationship with the poor demonstrates the reality of our claim to faith. Jesus willingly identified with the poor and oppressed, and expected his true followers to do the same. Doing nothing, or doing nothing but talking, are not options for us. We are called to do what we can, to bring a glimmer of hope into the darkest problems facing our globe, by showing compassion to those in need around us.

Rosie knew that her job as a social worker meant that most of her friends thought she had ticked the box when it came to "doing something". But she could only make a small, and usually only temporary, difference in the difficult conditions of the lives of the people she came across. The truth was, the terrible stories she came across on a daily basis gave her a taste of the scale of suffering around the world, and the statistics sickened her.

As Rosie read through the Facebook comments, she saw a word in a familiar verse that she had never noticed before: "Whatever you do for *one* of the least of these brothers and sisters of mine, you did for me." Rosie felt that God was speaking to her tonight.

She picked one cause where she felt her contribution would make a difference to at least one person, and prayed for one opportunity to offer one simple act of kindness to bring one glimmer of hope to somebody. One day at a time she would try to do something that made a small difference.

For further thought

BE: *reflection*. This chapter contained strong warnings about the dangers of neglecting to DO SOMETHING for Jesus. Reflect on whether you need to make some changes in light of the needs of the people around you.

SAY: *discussion*. "Can't sleep. Too many problems in the world. How can I help most effectively?"

How would you have answered Rosie's Facebook dilemma?

DO: *action*. Offer something from your kitchen or your wardrobe or extend an invitation to somebody who really needs it, or visit them.

CHAPTER 25

DO VIRAL

Graham was sneezing all over the place. As he sat at home
in quarantine from the outside world, he began to reflect on
his life. He had become a Christian in the army, and now, fifty
years on, with a career in engineering, and four children and
twelve grandchildren later, he still felt he had so much more
to give.

Retirement had been kind to him, and he had money and
time to spare, but he wondered if all of his reading, his
experiences, and the wisdom he had accrued over the years
were going to waste. He wondered again about writing his
memoirs, but even his own grandchildren were far more
interested in teaching him about their latest trends than they
were in learning about how life used to be.

He grabbed the Kleenex and the church magazine. He had
once been the editor, until it was felt that a younger person
could make it more relevant. But he wasn't ready to become
useless quite yet. Sneezes or no sneezes, he was going
to make some decisions today to pass on some of God's
blessings before it was too late.

Harry, aged three, and Charlie, aged one, are unlikely video
stars, but they are probably the most watched brothers in the

world. A 56-second clip of Charlie biting his brother's finger has been watched 490 million times.[1] That is 870 years' worth of viewing. It all began when their father shared the video with the boys' godfather, and then with a few other friends and family members. After a few weeks it had 200 views; after a few months it had several thousand; and within four years it had become the single most watched video clip ever, and synonymous with the Internet phenomenon known as the viral video.

It is not just videos that mimic the spread of infection over the Internet. In the summer of 2011, young people used social networks to organize riots across London, providing live updates to enable them to avoid or outnumber the police. It was also social networks that were used to organize thousands of volunteers to clean up the damage afterwards. Viral communication can be used to spread fun, violence or hope.[2] Jesus understood the power of social networks and encouraged his followers to redeem them and spread a good virus of grace around the world.

Christianity didn't just survive the death of its founder – it grew exponentially. From a tiny band of disciples in a forgotten corner of the Roman Empire, it grew to become the dominant global faith in just a few centuries. From eleven frightened disciples on a hill outside of Jerusalem, the church now officially extends to nearly a third of the population of the planet, with some 2.18 billion people claiming Christian faith.

Unlike viewing a video clip on YouTube, becoming a follower of Jesus involves much more than just pressing "Play" or "Like" on a website. In its early days (and still today in many places around the world),[3] it involved the costly decision to follow Jesus in the face of suffering and persecution. Indeed, Dietrich Bonheoffer, the German theologian, Second World War spy and Christian martyr, wrote: "When Christ calls a man, he bids him come and die… death in Jesus Christ, the death of the old man at his call."[4]

Christianity has thrived in the face of intense persecution and plagues. It has crossed class and cultural barriers. It is contagious, transforming everything it touches. Generation after generation has come to know the good news of Jesus. The key to this expansion[5] was Jesus' viral method of disciple making. But in an age and in cultures where viral marketing is becoming the norm, ironically, many Christians are becoming more reticent about "sharing" their faith. How can we recapture from Jesus the challenge to DO VIRAL again?

As Jesus was walking beside the Sea of Galilee, he saw two brothers, Simon called Peter and his brother Andrew. They were casting a net into the lake, for they were fishermen. "Come, follow me," Jesus said, "and I will send you out to fish for people." At once they left their nets and followed him.

Going on from there, he saw two other brothers, James son of Zebedee and his brother John. They were in a boat with their father Zebedee, preparing their nets. Jesus called them, and immediately they left the boat and their father and followed him.[6]

As the Son of God, Jesus didn't need any help to do his job; but in this passage at the beginning of Matthew's gospel, we see him hand-picking a bunch of guys to be his disciples. Jesus pours his life into his followers because it is through them that the gospel will travel virally throughout the world – transforming lives, cultures, countries and continents. From the call here in Matthew 4 to the last verse of this gospel, it is clear that making disciples is what Jesus is all about, and what he expects of his followers.

But it seems that someone forgot to tell Jesus how discipleship was supposed to work in the ancient world. Wannabe disciples were supposed to check out all the eligible rabbis and choose one,[7] rather like students picking which university to study at. But Jesus chose his own disciples, and he didn't go to the usual suspects to find them – he avoided the synagogue and the seminary and went to the seaside and the streets. Jesus picked unlikely, ordinary working people and invested a couple of years of his life into them. They were with him on the road and on the job. They saw his life up close and personal and up close and public. They saw the glory days and the dark days, the miracles and the misery, the busy times, the mealtimes and the downtimes.

But if Jesus, the Son of God and the perfect disciple-maker, needed three years of such intensive and intimate mentoring, teaching them both verbally and experientially, what chance have we got? How dare we try to disciple others as Jesus discipled? At the end of Matthew's gospel, we are told exactly why we dare.

After three years, the disciples knew Jesus well; but Jesus knew his disciples well too. He knew that for all his mentoring, they were still as doubtful and disorganized and dysfunctional as any of us. Yet Jesus still finished his last lesson to them with the Great Commission:

> *Then Jesus came to them and said, "All authority in heaven and on earth has been given to me. Therefore go and make disciples of all nations, baptizing them in the name of the Father and of the Son and of the Holy Spirit, and teaching them to obey everything I have commanded you. And surely I am with you always, to the very end of the age."*[8]

This passage is one of the most quoted parts of the New Testament, but the writer Dallas Willard refers to it as the "Great Omission",[9] because most of us use the passage as a proof text for evangelism and global mission, sadly missing its central thrust – which is, DO VIRAL disciple-making. The disciples of Jesus were commissioned to make disciples and teach them everything that he had commanded them, which necessarily includes the final command to make disciples. Jesus expected his disciples to make disciples to make disciples to make disciples and on and on virally until Kingdom come.[10] This process involves helping people find faith in Jesus Christ (i.e. evangelism), but overarching this is the command to help people find a fruitful, obedient, mature and viral faith in Jesus Christ (i.e. discipleship).

The Great Commission to make disciples is encouraging to us, not only because those unlikely, ordinary first disciples are so similar to us, with our flaws and failings, but also because of the resources Jesus puts at our disposal. We have authority: wherever we go, we have the backing of the Trinity – Father, Son and Spirit. And we also have the presence of Jesus – whenever we need it.

No, we are not the Son of God and the Saviour of the World, but the one and only Jesus has given us a clear challenge to take his message and go viral with it, ensuring that our relationship with him is contagious, daring to share our faith through our words and our lives, so that discipleship as a pattern is passed on down the generations, through history and to "the end of the world and the ends of the earth."[11]

As Graham sat at home, feeling like a caged tiger because of his flu, he began to pray for people in his church, writing down his prayers, as was his custom. There were so few things he had in common with the younger men and lads in his church, that many of his prayers were short, but as he wrote he noticed some points of connection.

Perhaps the sixth-former who always admired his old camera collection would like to have a few lessons in using them. Perhaps the stand-in preacher who often came round to browse through his bookshelves would like to borrow a couple of commentaries. Perhaps his grandson could teach him how to use the Internet to access his family tree. And perhaps in these contexts, he would be able to talk about a love for a Saviour that had persisted through five decades.

Graham had lots of hard-earned wisdom to pass on, from

how to make elderflower cordial to how to measure focal distance, from how to enjoy a daily prayer life to knowing when to hand over a ministry responsibility. The only thing Graham did not want to pass on was his cold.

For further thought

BE: *reflection.* Imagine a child refusing to share his new toy train. Why is he so afraid to lend it to his friend? What arguments does his father use to try to persuade him? Why does it make us smile to watch?

Now consider the reasons why we often find it so difficult to share our faith. Identify the reasons why we want to keep it for ourselves, and listen to our Father reasoning with us.

SAY: *discussion.* How can we, as a church, milk the wisdom from the older generations, and feed wisdom into the younger generations? How can we make discipleship contagious, sharing our faith, our lives, our burdens, our journeys?

DO: *action.* Look around your church community. Is there anyone you respect who you could ask to be mentored by? Is there anyone that you could get alongside to encourage?

CHAPTER 26

DO SABBATH

Monday, 7.35 p.m.

"We just don't feel we are getting anything out of the services any more. We feel tired all the time. Surely going to church should give you a bit of lift, but we are always the last ones to leave the service after we have packed away. We just think we need a time of receiving in church. If we could just hand over our responsibilities for a few months, we think it would change the way we relate to people in church. We understand it will leave a hole, but something has to give, as we are far too over-committed."

Jim had practised his speech a dozen times, and in ten minutes he was going to present it to his pastor. He hated letting people down, but he also hated going to church feeling resentful, so he knew he was doing the right thing. But it still sounded a bit self-centred. He looked at himself in the mirror and started again: "We just don't feel..."

We have a saying in our church: "We are a bit like a helicopter – don't come too close, in case you get sucked into the rotas!" Sundays are traditionally seen as a day for rest, but for many of us it is also the busiest day of the week. And for some people being busy in church services seems to suck the life out of them, and stop them getting closer to God. They want their day of rest, their Sabbath, back.

We have already considered the challenges of building Christ-ordained rhythms of responsibility and rest into our working days and our working lives. But how does the Sabbath principle fit into this? Is Sunday to be kept special by avoiding paid work, or soul-destroying tasks, or any kind of work, for that matter? Is the time in the week we set aside to do church sacrosanct? How do we DO SABBATH like Jesus? We are about to hear some challenges from Jesus, and they may not be quite what we are expecting:

> So, because Jesus was doing these things on the Sabbath, the Jewish leaders began to persecute him. In his defence Jesus said to them, "My Father is always at his work to this very day, and I too am working." For this reason they tried all the more to kill him; not only was he breaking the Sabbath, but he was even calling God his own Father, making himself equal with God.[1]

Breaking the Sabbath in first-century Israel was an indiscretion equivalent to a Nazi salute during the singing of "God Save the Queen" at a Remembrance Day Parade. The Jews had suffered for the sake of the fourth commandment, and to break it was tantamount to desecrating their heritage. It was no wonder that by breaking the Sabbath, Jesus' actions caused outrage amongst the Jewish authorities. What possible reason could he have had for deliberately causing such offence?

In order to help people in the first century know how to "keep the Sabbath", the religious leaders had piled up prohibitions and restrictions on what was and was not permissible on the seventh day of the week.[2] Their arbitrary and often hypocritical legal codes had developed and digressed to such a degree that by publicly healing a man who had been lame for thirty-eight years and lifting the burdens of his social isolation and physical disability, Jesus was considered to have very definitely crossed the line. The authorities came down on him like a ton of bricks and Jesus found himself at loggerheads with them over this very emotive subject. Was Jesus working? Had Jesus broken the law? Did he deserve to die?

Jesus' defence of his actions seemed to pour oil on the fire. "My Father is always at his work to this very day, and I, too, am working." There was no doubt that Jesus was not talking about Joseph fixing the odd table leg on the quiet after synagogue. The Jewish leaders understood immediately what his line of argument meant. They knew that Jesus was saying that he could not possibly be a lawbreaker, because in fact he was claiming to be The Lawmaker, God himself.

Imagine you saw a vehicle speeding, running red lights and driving on the wrong side of the road. You would be horrified. But if the driver got out and explained that he was a police officer attending an emergency, then that would put the matter in a whole different light. This is Jesus' logic: "I am not an ordinary human being. I am God in the flesh, so I have the right and the authority to follow my Father's example." The Jewish leaders refused to accept it – they now had Jesus on a secondary charge of blasphemy.

Was healing one man really worth this double jeopardy – not only participating in illegal activity but also making blasphemous claims, crimes that would lead to persecution, death threats and the death penalty? What lesson was Jesus so desperate to teach us?

The God who invented and championed the work/rest cycle and the Sabbath principle also challenges our priorities. Biblically, the concept of Sabbath is less about escaping the treadmill of everyday life, and more about bringing God's peace and rest to the whole of creation. Animals are rested, land is rested and people are rested, to help us to appreciate that we are no longer in captivity to slave-drivers.[3] In other words, the Sabbath helps us remember that our work does not rule over us, but rather, we keep control of the work that needs to be done.

BACK TO THE SOURCE

In light of this, Jesus' actions are not arbitrary transgressions. They bear no resemblance to my accidentally failing to stop at a red light because I am fiddling with my radio. Neither are they equivalent to my mischievous desire to stroll across the lawns every time I see a sign that says "Don't walk on the grass". However incensed Jesus was that God's clear commandment had been so confused by trivial and hypocritical laws stemming from the whim of some anal-retentive religious spoilsport, his healing was not some underhand sneer at their futility. Jesus' Sabbath-breaking healing was deliberately and provocatively aimed to bring us back to the heart of the Sabbath.

In the earlier chapter, "DO NOTHING", we saw that Mark's gospel records seven occasions when Jesus rested. The gospels also include seven occasions when Jesus healed on the Sabbath. He heals a man with a withered hand,[4] a crippled woman,[5] a man who had been paralysed for thirty-eight years,[6] Peter's mother-in-law,[7] and a man born blind;[8] and he drives out demons[9] and he feeds the hungry,[10] all on Sabbath days. By breaking through the religious ritualistic norms and smashing their taboos, Jesus shows us that the Sabbath is all about ushering in God's Kingdom and bringing rest to others. In fact, the coming of the Kingdom is described in Hebrews as entering the "Sabbath-rest for the people of God".[11] The healings are a foretaste of the final Sabbath day that is yet to come, the time when there will be no more sickness or hunger, but a state of permanent peace and rest over all creation.

As we are being challenged to BE, SAY and DO like Jesus, it may seem strange that there is no chapter about being part of a local church. Jesus walked the planet before the Christian church was founded, but it is in these last two chapters that we come closest to understanding how Jesus would have done church. First, we looked at his intentional, intimate and intensive strategy of virally sharing the faith, and now we have seen his involved, inclusive and industrious attitude to sharing the peace.

To help us DO SABBATH like Jesus, we need to remember three things. First, the Sabbath is a gift to us from God, and is supposed to give us a foretaste of the rest that awaits us in the presence of God in heaven. We are supposed to enjoy it. Secondly, this gift is not only for us, but for all – and like Jesus and our heavenly Father, we may need to work hard to make sure that gift gets to the recipients who really need it. Looking to those in our congregation and in our community who need Sabbath rest can help us become like Jesus, honour Jesus and draw others to Jesus. Finally, observing the Sabbath in these two ways – both receiving and giving – helps us to visibly demonstrate our love for God and to offer him our gift of worship.

"We just don't feel..." Jim stopped himself mid-sentence. He especially didn't like his wife feeling stressed on a Sunday, but no matter how he looked at it, or how he phrased it, he knew they were being entirely selfish. If they gave up some of their responsibilities, they were effectively loading more onto already busy people – people they loved and cared about, and people who had given generously to them.

Instead, he told his pastor how he felt. He wanted to serve at church, but didn't want to do it resentfully. He wanted to use the gifts God had given him to bless others, but felt like his own batteries needed to be recharged somewhere along the line too. He wanted to know whether he needed to change his heart attitude, or his responsibilities at church, or any other area of his life that was blocking his freedom to give.

As they talked long into the evening, the burden began to be lifted, a fresh perspective began to shine through, some practical steps forward were planned, and his church became even more precious.

For further thought

BE: *reflection*. How might seeing the Sabbath principle as an opportunity to both give and receive, work and rest, change the way you spend your Sundays?

SAY: *discussion*. If you were Jim's pastor, what advice would you give him in light of the needs of the wider community?

DO: *action*. In your church community, who is in most need of some rest and relief? Would a cooked meal, or an offer of babysitting, or a lift to an appointment help? Plan something practical as a gift to them.

CHAPTER 27

DO MIRACLES

Whatever the doctors had said with their long words and medical terms and options and sympathies and paperwork, Joy understood perfectly what they meant: her son was dying. They had been very kind, but also very clear that Dylan's months, if not days, were numbered. The cancer was aggressive, and because he was so young, it had spread more quickly, and they were running out of interventions.

Joy, sitting at his bedside while he was sedated, felt numb. She could not accept this terrible prognosis. One of the doctors had said that they needed a miracle, and so a miracle was what she was going to ask for.

But she had never really believed that God worked like that in the twenty-first century. She had always said she would rather be sceptical than gullible. But at this point she would do anything if it meant saving her son.

Ask the average shopper in the street, "What did Jesus do?" and miracles are going to come high up on their list. A significant proportion of the gospels is made up of miracle accounts and hardly a page goes by without one being performed. We are also told that Jesus performed many more miracles that were not included in the gospels.[1] And yet for the average Christian, many a year goes by without one.

There may be many reasons for this – our self-sufficiency, our perspective, our needs, our church styles, even our theology. As with so much of the Christian faith, there is a range of views as to just how far we can emulate Jesus and DO MIRACLES. Let's look at the two extreme ends of the scale.

At one end there are those who argue that God never intervenes miraculously. Cessationists[2] tend to believe that the miracles marked Jesus out as the Son of God, and to a lesser extent they also ratified the ministry of Jesus' chosen apostles. Miracles acted as an identification mark in the days before Scripture[3] was available to point us to God.

At the other end there are those who take literally Jesus' promise that "they will do even greater things than these"[4] and expect miracles of healing more frequently even than we hear about in the gospels. Sometimes, those at this end of the spectrum also believe that if the miracles are in short supply, the problem may well lie with the Christian's level of faith, level of sin or level of prayer.[5]

Many Christians fall somewhere between these two positions, often believing, in theory, that God can perform miracles through us, but not seeing this in practice in our communities as often as we would like. Without going any deeper into the arguments for and against the different permutations of these positions, let us look at what the following Bible passage seems to indicate and find some principles we can agree on:

> When they found him on the other side of the lake, they asked him, "Rabbi, when did you get here?"
>
> Jesus answered, "Very truly I tell you, you are looking for me, not because you saw the signs I performed but because you ate the loaves and had your fill. Do not work for food that spoils, but for food that endures to eternal life, which the Son of Man will give you. On him God the Father has placed his seal of approval."
>
> Then they asked him, "What must we do to do the works God requires?"

Jesus answered, "The work of God is this: to believe in the one he has sent."

So they asked him, "What sign then will you give that we may see it and believe you? What will you do? Our ancestors ate the manna in the wilderness; as it is written: 'He gave them bread from heaven to eat.'"

Jesus said to them, "Very truly I tell you, it is not Moses who has given you the bread from heaven, but it is my Father who gives you the true bread from heaven. For the bread of God is the bread that comes down from heaven and gives life to the world."[6]

Here are three observations from this subtle passage:

First, Jesus taught that miracles do not guarantee faith. The crowds that gathered around Jesus seemed more interested in the free meal itself, than how it had appeared. They remind me of my dog Brady, who would walk beside me down the street without any need for a leash, but once we got to the park he would abandon me to make friends with anyone that would offer to share their lunch with him. We are equally in danger of allowing our affection for and loyalty to Jesus to be based solely on getting our needs met, loving him for what he does for us, not for who he is.

Secondly, the miracle was pointing to something beyond simply meeting the immediate need. Jesus had compassion on the crowd and met their physical need for sustenance, but the miracle was also a sign. I remember being on a beach with Brady once and using my finger to draw his attention to a pile of sticks on the shoreline. He cocked his head to one side in an effort to appear like he was trying to understand, but simply looked at my finger. No matter how hard I tried, I could not get him to look at what I was pointing at. Similarly, the miraculous provision of food was supposed to point people to Jesus' identity, but sadly, the crowd saw only the temporary bread and fish and not the one who is the "Bread of Life" standing in front of them.

Thirdly, sometimes even Jesus refused to perform a miracle. When the crowd asked directly for a sign, Jesus declined to give them one. His argument was that there was more than enough evidence to go on already: Moses and the manna in the wilderness; Jesus and the bread on the mountainside. The parallels were unmissable.[7] Jesus could be no other than the ultimate sign himself, the promised Messiah and the Bread from Heaven. To ignore Jesus and focus on the miracles is like meeting the Queen in person but ignoring her to focus on her image on the coins in your hand as you work out if you can afford a panini at Costa Coffee.

God may or may not answer our prayers for miracles, and even when he does provide them, they may or may not help us draw closer to Jesus, but at the end of the day, understanding who Jesus really is trumps anything a miracle may achieve. The New Testament promises that miracles will cease one day when "completeness comes" and we see Christ "face to face".[8] Some Christians believe this cessation happened when the New Testament was written. Others, myself included, believe it will happen at the end of human history when we get to see Jesus face to face.

In light of this grey area, we are certainly at liberty to ask God for a miracle, knowing he is perfectly capable of intervening. There is no embarrassment in asking because it is an acknowledgment of both his power and his overriding control of the situation, and he has commanded us to bring our anxieties and requests to him in prayer. But we ask; we do not demand. Prayer is a request to the almighty God, not an almighty command. In the end it is God, not us, who decides if a miracle is an appropriate response to the situation.

Faith is trusting that he can, not demanding that he will. Faith is trusting that God is good, despite the bad circumstances; faith is not dependent on good circumstances. Faith is saying, "Only if you will it", not "Only if you do it".

If no miracle occurs, we are allowed to feel frustrated. The Psalms are full of heartfelt, woeful prayers of distress and disappointment.[9] We don't need to blame ourselves for lack of faith – God sometimes does withhold healings and miracles, not because he has been defeated by our circumstances or because he is uncaring about our pain, but because he knows what is ultimately best for our faith and the faith of others.

There are glimpses in the Old Testament of this kind of trust. When Shadrach and his friends are about to be thrown into the fiery furnace, they entrust themselves to God with a courageous speech on the way to facing incineration:

> *If the God we serve is able to deliver us, then he will deliver us*
> *from the blazing furnace and from Your Majesty's hand. But even*
> *if he does not, we want you to know, Your Majesty, that we will*
> *not serve your gods or worship the image of gold you have set up.*[10]

Or take another example, from the book of Habakkuk:

> *Though the fig tree does not bud*
> *and there are no grapes on the vines,*
> *though the olive crop fails*
> *and the fields produce no food,*
> *though there are no sheep in the pen*
> *and no cattle in the stalls,*
> *yet I will rejoice in the Lord,*
> *I will be joyful in God my Saviour.*[11]

I would love to DO MIRACLES like Jesus, but only Jesus can do miracles. We can ask him to intervene miraculously in and through our lives, but ultimately what Jesus challenges us to do is to learn to trust God, whatever our circumstances, and to help others when trusting God is painfully difficult. Sometimes even this requires a miracle, one which God is more than willing to help us with.

Joy picked up the Gideon Bible from the bedside table and read again the miracle of the raising of Jairus' daughter. How she wished Jesus had chosen to be born in Watford thirty years ago rather than Bethlehem two millennia ago. She would have earnestly pleaded with Jesus too, and called on him to take care of her son, to bring him back to her.

She pictured Dylan waking up in Jesus' arms, restored to life, the cancer gone, and the two of them disappearing into the kitchen to get some bread and soup. That was what she wanted more than anything else in the world. Would it be her kitchen at home or heaven's kitchen?

She was going to pray hard for a miracle for her son, either way; and for a miracle for herself, that she would have the faith to trust Jesus, whatever happened.

For further thought

BE: *reflection*. What miracle would you love Jesus to perform today? Spend some time praying into that situation, recognizing God's ultimate power and righteousness. Use some of the Scripture verses in this chapter to help your prayers.

SAY: *discussion*. Read the account of Thomas's doubt in John 20:24–29. What is the link between miracles, blessings and faith, according to these verses? How does this correspond with your own experiences?

DO: *action*. Rewrite the Habakkuk passage in your own words, referring to the crises and anxieties facing you at the moment. Display it somewhere where you can read it often and develop this kind of trust and joy in God our Saviour.

CHAPTER 28

DO REVOLUTION

Wednesday, 8.10 a.m.

Raj was wound up like a coiled spring. The email from his local MP was the antithesis of what he had expected. Instead of offering assurances of understanding and promises of support, the MP had not only refused to listen to any of the points Raj had raised, but had also refused to help him. On top of that, he had even gone on the offensive, making not-so-subtle threats against Raj that could get him into a lot of trouble at work. Raj was angry. And when he heard that a close friend in an even worse situation than him had been on the receiving end of a similarly aggressive ultimatum, he was livid.

Option number one was to go to the papers and publish the incriminating evidence to put an end to the serial bullying. But the MP was a powerful man, and if this was how he responded to a cry for help, how would he respond to a squealer? Option number two was to try a more softly, softly approach, trying to win the guy over by persistently gracious responses. As if! Option three was to get electioneering and depose the MP democratically by getting himself elected in his place: "Vote for Raj, your non-bullying MP!" Option four was to turn the other cheek and move on with his life.

He wanted to DO REVOLUTION, but the only revolving going on was these options going round and round in his head. What would Jesus do?

Talking about revolution, what battles do you find yourself fighting over and over? An insensitive neighbour? A persistent temptation? An issue in the workplace? An attitude at church? The daily routine? Does it ever feel like you are fighting the same battles over and over and getting nowhere? Like a song stuck on repeat? Like the curse of Sisyphus, meaninglessly pushing his boulder up the mountain, only for it to roll back to the starting point? Those French existentialist philosophers had a point: the human condition does seem to get stuck with these spin cycles of remorseless repetition that destroy our dreams and aspirations. Whether you want to launch a political revolution in your town or a personal revolution in your life, there's no one better to learn from than Jesus the revolutionary.

Jesus is the most revolutionary person in history. Rather than settling into the cycle of relentless routines, Jesus' life seems to be a continual adventure. It is hard to find an ordinary day in his life: one day he is at a high-society dinner, the next he is fraternizing with the drop-outs of society; one moment he is preaching on a hillside, the next he is calming a raging storm. There seems to be no repeat mode in Jesus' lifestyle. He does the most radical and unpredictable things, like exposing injustice and hypocrisy, talking to prostitutes, touching lepers – even talking to trees...

The next day as they were leaving Bethany, Jesus was hungry.
Seeing in the distance a fig tree in leaf, he went to find out if it had
any fruit. When he reached it, he found nothing but leaves, because
it was not the season for figs. Then he said to the tree, "May no one
ever eat fruit from you again." And his disciples heard him say it.

On reaching Jerusalem, Jesus entered the temple courts and
began driving out those who were buying and selling there. He
overturned the tables of the money changers and the benches
of those selling doves, and would not allow anyone to carry
merchandise through the temple courts. And as he taught them, he

said, "Is it not written: 'My house will be called a house of prayer for all nations'? But you have made it 'a den of robbers'."[1]

Talk about revolution! Jesus certainly turned things over. No mild-mannered Messiah here. Jesus finds the business of the corrupt money-changers and dove-sellers revolting, so he turns the tables on them and sends them packing, driving them out with a whip.[2] Is this really the way Jesus wants us to revolutionize our towns and churches – with acts of violence and vandalism and vendetta? Or does Jesus get away with this seemingly uncharacteristic outburst because he is the Son of God and the Saviour of the World? How are we supposed to understand this passage and apply it to the problems we face in our lives so we can DO REVOLUTION like Jesus?

To begin finding answers to these questions, we need to look for clues as to what provoked Jesus in the first place. Just the day before, the crowds came out to meet and greet him with palm branches and cheers. But the very next day he seems unusually short-tempered as he looks for fresh figs to satisfy his hunger. When he discovers that the tree is barren, he verbally condemns the tree, before going back to Jerusalem to physically condemn the money-changers.

At first sight, both the cursing of the tree and the clearing of the temple seem too irrational and hot-headed for Jesus. But this was not Jesus having a bad day. He was not taking out his frustrations. He was not acting out of character. Mark deliberately juxtaposes these two events to explain to us the logic behind Jesus' anger.

Fig trees, like olive trees and vines, are prolific in Israel and are used frequently in the Old Testament as a symbol for the nation.[3] When Jesus approaches this fig tree, he finds it looks healthy on the outside, but is totally lacking in fruit, exactly as he is finding the nation of Israel. When he enters the temple, another national symbol, he finds the hustle and bustle he expects, but looking closer, he finds not worship but commerce. Moreover, the tradesmen had entirely taken over the particular zone of the temple dedicated as a place of sanctuary for the Gentiles to come and discover and worship God. The busyness and business meant that the Gentiles were effectively banished. Jesus' eviction of the money-changers mirrors their own eviction of the Gentiles.

This attack is not out of character for a God who desires to make room for all nations to hear of his love and compassion, and invites them in rather than shutting them out. This attack is not out of character for Jesus, who is similarly morally incensed when he hears about how some people are finding a way to lead young children away from God. He explains clearly that this is utterly unacceptable: "And if anyone causes one of these little ones who believe in me to sin, it would be better for him to be thrown into the sea with a large millstone tied around his neck."[4]

These harsh words, like Jesus' harsh actions in the temple courts, are driven by his compassion. Jesus will not tolerate anyone blocking others from experiencing the love of God in their lives. Gentiles, children, the rejects of society are welcomed into the Kingdom, and those who seek to stand in their way are judged severely.

Jesus is incensed. He humiliates the money-changers and sends them packing. Perhaps his roughness is a mercy. I can imagine it caused quite a stir. As J. R. Edwards comments, the Jews expected their Messiah to rid Israel of its troublesome Gentile invaders, to "purge Jerusalem and the temple of Gentiles, aliens, and foreigners... Jesus' action, however, is exactly the reverse. He does not clear the temple of Gentiles, but for them."[5]

When Jesus did revolution, he did not just overturn the tables, but overhauled long-held prejudices and practices. His revolution was not about bullying his way into power, or making a name for himself, but about love and mercy and championing the cause and the case of the poor, the outcast and the marginalized. To DO REVOLUTION like Jesus means rousing the church to action, ensuring the outsiders are welcomed, overhauling our own prejudices, living up to our calling.

Raj could have stayed stuck in his cycle of decision making for a long time. He was a bit like that – he had taken so long to decide whether to propose over a romantic dinner or on the London Eye or on Brighton Pier, that his then girlfriend ended up doing the job for him at Elephant and Castle Tube Station.

This time he was going to stand up for the truth and grasp the proverbial nettle with both hands, and hope he didn't get stung. It would be a personal revolution – as his fiancée would testify – and maybe even the start of a spiritual revolution as he stepped out in faith. He also prayed it would turn the tables on the self-important Member of Parliament, with his threats and ultimatums.

So option two it was, then... Or maybe option four...?

For further thought

BE: *reflection*. Read Matthew 18, where Jesus teaches us to be rough and ruthless and revolutionary with the sins in our own lives. What does this mean in your own life?

SAY: *discussion*. The practice of commerce in the temple had become part of the status quo, unquestioned by the worshippers or the religious leaders. Is there anything like that in our churches which is accepted as normal, but which is effectively banishing those who really need to hear our gospel? How far are you prepared to change?

DO: *action*. Visit some of the "unwelcome" people in your neighbourhood. Ask them what would make it easier for them to come to church. Then do something with that information – make some changes, invite the outcasts, start a revolution.

CHAPTER 29

DO TOUCH

He woke up from another nightmare. When Orlando had finally agreed to serve at church, his pastor had added him to the welcome team. He had no idea just what awkward predicaments awaited him.

He was supposed to smile and shake people's hands, simultaneously offering a greeting and a notice sheet. No mean feat for someone who got thrown out of drum lessons at the age of seven – after just one lesson. When visitors who didn't know the unspoken drill arrived and ended up shaking the notice sheet instead of his hand, he felt like one of his church foyer nightmares was coming true.

There were a few church members he dreaded too. There were a few who liked kissing, and he could never remember who did one cheek and who did both, or whether it was right or left cheek first, or who wanted an air peck and who nuzzled in for the full smacker, and what on earth he was supposed to do when they left traces of saliva or lipstick.

Even worse were those who seemed intent on trying to squeeze the life out of him. Being below average height meant that he often got folded directly into someone's armpit as they man-hugged their pleasure at being back in church. It was all terribly tactile for him, really.

After only a few weeks, he had made up his mind: he was going to ask to be reassigned to a "behind" position – behind a sound-desk, behind a kitchen hatch, or behind the free literature table.

To the untrained eye it doesn't look like much – just a bunch of dots. Not in a Jackson Pollock splatter kind of arrangement, but an orderly linear structure of embossed spots. To really see the meaning and the humour of this piece of art, you have to be blind. When Braille readers pass their fingertips over the surface you see them smile: "Do not touch," they read. The irony is that only those who touch are informed that touching is not permitted.

But this is not the only invisible "Do not touch" sign in our culture. When I take my children into our local stationers, the lady behind the counter sends out a "Do not touch!" command with her eyes. At work I know that when I see a sandwich in the fridge with a name sticker attached to the cellophane, it effectively shouts, "Do not touch!" When I stand on a crowded underground train and am uncomfortably close to a guy building an invisible force field with his iPod and book, I strain all sorts of muscles to ensure I do not have any actual physical contact and break his "Do not touch" aura.

Jesus built up a reputation as someone who was not afraid either to touch or be touched. He touched the culturally untouchable lepers, and when the woman who was ceremonially unclean because of her bleeding touched him secretly, he acknowledged her and healed her. The following story is another powerful example of Jesus' intentional and inspirational touch:

Soon afterward, Jesus went to a town called Nain, and his disciples and a large crowd went along with him. As he approached the town gate, a dead person was being carried out – the only son of his mother, and she was a widow. And a large crowd from the town was with her. When the Lord saw her, his heart went out to her and he said, "Don't cry."

Then he went up and touched the bier they were carrying him on, and the bearers stood still. He said, "Young man, I say to you, get up!" The dead man sat up and began to talk, and Jesus gave him back to his mother.

They were all filled with awe and praised God.[1]

Jesus is more than capable of long-distance healings. In fact he does so in the verses just prior to this incident, to heal the servant of a Roman centurion. But why does he not do this all the time? It would have saved an awful lot of travelling, saved some controversy (especially in the case of a Jew entering a Gentile home), and saved him from getting his hands dirty. In this passage he has things to do and places to be, and is held up by a funeral procession, so a quick distance-healing would have cleared the road nicely. Instead Jesus stops to talk to the woman who has experienced a double tragedy, losing both her husband and her only son.

The first thing to notice here is that the plight of the desolate woman touches Jesus, and his heart goes out to her in compassion and sympathy. He allows the situation to touch him to such an extent that the miracle is portrayed more as the healing of the widow from her distress, than the raising of a child from the dead.[2] This is highlighted as we are told that Jesus "gave him back to his mother".

The second observation is that after the woman's plight touches Jesus, he touches the coffin. If a stranger dared to join the pall-bearers in a family funeral today, it would be considered extremely inappropriate. But Jesus takes time to talk to the bereaved family and joins with the mourners. His intervention in this funeral is not as a stranger, but as a sympathizer. It's not a hands-off affair, it's a picture of heart felt, hands-on compassion. We may have expected this at Lazarus' funeral, as he was a valued friend, but Jesus' compassion is not restricted to his circle of friends. He is not untouched by a stranger's funeral.

It's not as though Jesus *needs* to touch the coffin to perform the miracle. At Lazarus' funeral, Jesus asked others to move the stone away and then commanded the corpse to life with a loud voice.[3] So why does Jesus have physical contact with the dead this time? One view is that it was a deliberate transgression of the prohibitions in the book of Numbers,[4] making himself ceremonially unclean in the process, to reinforce his identification with the mourners.

When Jesus halts the funeral procession, it is a very visual reminder that he has the power to stop death itself, and turn mourning into dancing. And when Jesus touches the coffin, it is not he who gets contaminated by death, but rather the dead who get resurrected by Jesus. When he touches the lepers he is not infected; instead they are cleansed. When he is touched by the woman with the flow of blood, he is not made unclean; instead she is restored. His touch is an expression of his identification with the distressed, of his deep compassion, of his contagious purity, and of his total power.

How can we DO TOUCH like Jesus, even though we are not Jesus? How can we DO TOUCH like Jesus in a culture of invisible "Do not touch" signs? Here are a few challenges for us to consider.

Social media bring with them all sorts of advantages: we can mobilize, confer and collaborate with a far wider group of people than our ancestors could ever dream of. We can stay "in touch" more easily with so many more acquaintances, but we don't touch them. Due to busy schedules, I spend more time communicating with my next-door neighbour on Facebook than I do face to face. How can we ensure that being in touch is not a substitute for DO TOUCH?

We are more than capable of doing long-distance empathy[5] when faced with news and images of earthquakes, hurricanes or famines, but how can we ensure they touch us to such an extent that we are prepared to stop what we are doing and get involved rather than develop "compassion fatigue"?[6]

Should we learn something from the first-century church, who washed one another's feet, laid hands on the sick, greeted one another with a holy kiss, or extended the right hand of fellowship? Could this embodied, physical affection that Christians were supposed to practise when together back then, be of increasing significance in our ever more atomistic and alienated society?

In our churches today, where many people bear the scars of inappropriate and abusive physical contact, how can we uphold vital child protection policies and practices, and still be willing to break the cultural taboos of touching the untouchable in ways that bring wholeness and healing?

Orlando's pastor smiled knowingly. He much preferred being behind the pulpit than getting his hands dirty in the messy lives of his congregation. He listened for a while and then refused Orlando's request for a transfer to a "behind" job. However awkward Orlando felt offering his hand for a handshake, or his cheek for a kiss, the pastor encouraged him to see it as an act of service, passing on God's love and value to whoever walked through that door.

For further thought

BE: *reflection*. How comfortable are you offering and receiving physical contact? Can you think of times in your week when some level of appropriate physical contact could communicate sympathy or affection or healing?

SAY: *discussion*. To what extent do you think society is changing to remove all need of physical contact in our day-to-day lives? For example, you can self-serve at the supermarket, petrol station and library, or order your clothes, books and food online.

Do you think these shifts are good or bad? How should the church respond?

DO: *action.* Choose one of the following to try out in your home group as a symbol of your willingness to be touched by one another and to carry one another's burdens: foot-washing, laying on of hands, greeting with a holy kiss, giving the right hand of fellowship.

CHAPTER 30

DO TOGETHER

Friday, 7 p.m.

Akin was reading a book that his friend Emily had bought him. It was a great read, with plenty of intriguing stories and thirty challenges for him to be, do and say like Jesus, and now he was about to finish off the last chapter. But he felt uneasy.

First, he had hoped this book would transform his life forever. He always started books with the expectation that this next one would solve the riddle of his Christian life, unlock resources that he didn't know anything about, and lift him onto a higher spiritual plain. But now he only had one chapter left, and was worried that these last pages would not be able to fix it all for him.

Secondly, the more he read the book, the more he wanted to be like Jesus, speak like him and act like him, and yet also the more aware he was of his own inadequacy. He had learned a lot during the thirty challenges, but part of him felt that if it was a test, he would have scored zero.

Thirdly, Akin was seeing Emily later tonight, and she was bound to ask him if her gift was the life-changing book he had been searching for. What would he say?

The chairs have been set out, the urn switched on, the sound system rigged and tested, the notice sheets folded, the cakes

176

and fruit laid out, the heating turned up, the Bibles distributed, the instruments tuned. The congregation arrives and we are asked to close our eyes and focus on Jesus. All that work to prepare for a gathering – now I have to pretend I am on my own! I could do that in the comfort of my home without all the palaver of set-up duties. It is no wonder many people are opting out of church services altogether and listening to their favourite worship CDs and taking their pick of online preaching instead. Why settle for an average preacher, an average worship band, a load of rotas and a motley crew of fellow worshippers, when you could be listening to world-class preachers and worship leaders in the comfort of your home?

Jesus had the most intimate relationship with his Father God, and the most astute understanding of Scripture that anyone on earth ever had, but he never spoke those universal church leader cliché words: "I don't know what sort of week you have had, but please close your eyes and focus now on God." Quite the opposite – almost everything Jesus did, he would DO TOGETHER with others. And the Bible clearly teaches that we too need other believers around us so we can DO TOGETHER our faith, our worship, and our service.

For those of us tempted to try to fix our spiritual lives by ourselves, we could perhaps be both comforted and challenged by the following passage:

The seventy-two returned with joy and said, "Lord, even the demons submit to us in your name."

He replied, "I saw Satan fall like lightning from heaven. I have given you authority to trample on snakes and scorpions and to overcome all the power of the enemy; nothing will harm you. However, do not rejoice that the spirits submit to you, but rejoice that your names are written in heaven."

At that time Jesus, full of joy through the Holy Spirit, said, "I praise you, Father, Lord of heaven and earth, because you have

*hidden these things from the wise and learned, and revealed them
to little children. Yes, Father, for this was your good pleasure."*[1]

The sending out of the seventy-two is a bit of a puzzle. Only
Luke, of the four gospel writers, includes the mission of the
seventy-two.[2] We don't really know where everyone came
from, when Jesus recruited them or where they went to after
this episode. However, the account is significant, because here,
near the beginning of Jesus' ministry, he is already setting up
some principles for us believers as we DO TOGETHER what
Jesus sends us to do.

First, Jesus was not arbitrary with his numbers. Just as his
twelve disciples mirrored the twelve tribes of Israel, signifying
the renewal of God's people, the seventy-two disciples of this
passage mirrored the number of nations that are listed in the
table of nations in Genesis 10.[3] Jesus was indicating that his
message and his mission would go not only to the borders of
Israel, but beyond, to bring renewal to the whole planet. They
were sent out not by themselves, but with company.

Secondly, this key aspect of hospitality and relationship is
part and parcel of the message. Jesus' messengers were given
very specific instructions, particularly regarding the hospitality
they were to receive. In fact, if Jesus' six dozen missionaries
were not received warmly, they were to wipe the dust off their
feet with a final warning: "The kingdom of God has come
near to you."[4] To refuse hospitality to Jesus' messengers was
tantamount to rejecting the Kingdom of God. Jesus chose to use
people to be the means through which others would come to
know God. The missiologist Lesslie Newbigin argued that this
was God's chosen method right back to the time of Abraham,
when if anyone wanted to know God, they had to get to know
his people, the bearers of his blessing to all the nations.[5] This
method is constant. Everyone who gets connected with God
as a Heavenly Father is also simultaneously welcomed into a
whole family of believers.

These two principles of mission together and hospitality together are introduced right at the beginning of Jesus' discipleship ministry, and we are left in no doubt that the call to discipleship will be difficult with respect to both mission and hospitality. As for the mission, we are to expect to feel like "lambs among wolves",[6] and as for the hospitality, we are told that we are as likely to be rejected as we are to be accepted. In fact, Jesus warns, "the hour is coming when those who kill you will think they are offering a service to God."[7] As we walk in the footsteps of the seventy-two, no matter how many books we read or conferences we attend or podcasts we listen to or church services we serve at, our mission together will still be costly, difficult and dangerous.

However, we are also assured that whether we face difficulties or enjoy successes, our value is not based on these. After experiencing the authority of Jesus working through them, the seventy-two return jubilant from their short-term mission trip. Jesus cautions them. The lambs that had been sent out amongst lambs are not to rejoice over the spiritual victories, but are to rejoice because their names are written in "the Lamb's book of life".[8] Why this caution? It feels like a referee preventing a player from celebrating after scoring a goal. But Jesus needs to remind us to celebrate what is more important and more enduring. For those times when we struggle to see results either in our personal lives or in our ministry with others, we can still know that ultimately Jesus, the Lamb of God, secures our salvation.

We have a role in God's big plans. We go with his authority, but we go in weakness into dangerous territory. We go with his message of grace, and we also go to minister grace to others. Sometimes we will see God working powerfully through us. Sometimes we will be rejected and sent packing. But wherever we go, we go together. Our church family are our travelling companions for now and beyond into eternity.

The problem with the idea that you can do church on your own with an iPod is that church was never supposed to consist of a minimum weekly dose of worship and teaching. The church is supposed to be a missionary community sent into dangerous territory in the authority of Jesus but following in the footsteps of a crucified Messiah. We were sent into the world with a revolutionary message to demonstrate and speak out about the coming King Jesus. This message is so powerful that, out of fear, the resistance to it will be severe. But we are not alone. We go with the power and authority and company of Jesus, and with the help and support and company of our brothers and sisters. If we are going to be like Jesus, say like Jesus and do like Jesus, we need all the help we can get. DO TOGETHER.

Akin took comfort in the fact that God was not scoring his life out of thirty. He was not supposed to measure up to a checklist in this book he had just finished, because he knew of a far superior book. His name was written in the Lamb's book of life because of Jesus' achievements, not his. He recognized that his weaknesses made him more dependent on God and on other believers. He was very grateful to Emily for caring about his spiritual health, and decided to pass the book on to their mutual friend Dyfed, who he had been praying for recently. Perhaps TOGETHER they would be able to work out which areas they could work on. Perhaps little by little, TOGETHER they would be able to BE, SAY, DO like their Lord and Saviour, Jesus Christ.

For further thought

BE: *reflection*. When do you feel like a lamb amongst wolves, and when do you feel like a scorpion-and-snake-trampler? What makes you feel encouraged or discouraged in your Christian life? Compare these things with the fact that your name is written in the Lamb's book of life.

SAY: *discussion*. Your church probably has many faults, but what are the top ten things you are grateful for as part of a Christian family or community? How can you express your gratitude for them today?

DO: *action*. Pick one of the challenges in this book to work on together with a Christian friend.

NOTES

Introduction

1. "Muscle memory is not a memory stored in your muscles, of course, but memories stored in your brain that are much like a cache of frequently enacted tasks for your muscles. It's a form of procedural memory that can help you become very good at something through repetition, but in exactly the same way it can make you absolutely terrible at that same thing." http://lifehacker.com/5799234/how-muscle-memory-works-and-how-it-affects-your-success

2. Moral philosophers call this virtue. See N. T. Wright, *After Virtue*, SPCK, 2010.

1. Be Iconic

1. See J. Baggini, *The Pig that Wants to be Eaten, and Ninety-nine Other Thought Experiments*, Granta Books, 2010.

2. Genesis 1:26.

3. S. McKnight, *Embracing Grace: A Gospel for All of Us*, Paraclete Press, 2009, p. 18.

4. Genesis 9:6.

5. Colossians 1:15.

6. A. F. Holmes, *Contours of Christian Philosophy: Ethics – Approaching Moral Decisions*, IVP, 1984, p. 85.

2. Be Glorious

1. Romans 3:23.

2. 2 Corinthians 3:17–18.

3. You may sense here a mediating position between John Piper and N. T. Wright's views on justification. See the lecture by K. Vanhoozer, "Wrighting the Wrongs of the Reformation", presented at Wheaton College, 17/4/10, for more on this theme.

4. Exodus 34:6–7.

5. Galatians 5:22–23.

6. Hebrews 1:1–3.

7. For more on habit-forming creating a virtuous character, see N. T. Wright, *After Virtue*, SPCK, 2010.

3. Be True

1. For an exploration of popular artistic impressions of Jesus, see A. Hirsch and M. Frost, *Jesus: A wild messiah for a missional church*, Hendrickson, 2009, pp. 104ff.

2. Best Friend Forever.

3. This idea of projecting onto Jesus is the age-old challenge of the correct relationship between relating the gospel to our culture. This chapter outlines some basic ways in which the gospel message can be accommodated to fit in with cultural norms. This is often known as syncretism. See A. E. Walls, "The Gospel as Prisoner and Liberator of Culture", in A. E. Walls, *The Missionary Movement in Christian History: Studies in the transmission of faith*, Edinburgh: T. & T. Clark, 1996, pp. 3–15, first published in *Faith and Thought*, 108 (1 & 2), 1982, pp. 39–52.

4. See C. R. Padilla, *Mission Between the Times*, Eerdmans, 1985, p. 88.

5. D. Bosch, "Witness to the World – Christian Mission in Theological Perspective", *New Foundations Theological Library*, Atlanta: John Knox Press, 1980, p. 202.

6. N. T. Wright, *Colossians and Philemon: An introduction and commentary*, Tyndale New Testament Commentaries, Nottingham, England: Inter-Varsity Press, 1986.

7. Colossians 1:15–20.

8. B. J. Walsh and S. Keesmat, *Colossians Remixed: Subverting the empire*, IVP, 2004, p. 84.

9. When John uses the term *Logos* in the prologue to his gospel, he is employing the same idea of Jesus as "the unifying, rational principle holding together a world in perpetual flux". S. B. Ferguson and J. Packer, *New Dictionary of Theology* (electronic ed.), Downers Grove, IL: InterVarsity Press, 2000, p. 395.

10. D. Bonhoeffer, *Letters and Papers from Prison*, Fontana, 1959, p. 173.

4. Be Down to Earth

1. See John 3:17–18.

2. To see John's gospel through the lens of swapping, see K. Kandiah, *Life Swap: Finding the life you always wanted*, Monarch, 2006.

3. Matthew 2:18.

4. John 20:19–21.

5. For more on this theme of mission as peacemaking, see S. B. Bevans and R. P. Schroeder, *Constants in Context: A Theology of Mission for Today*, Orbis, 2004, pp. 373–4.

6. D. Bosch, *Transforming Mission*, Orbis, 1991, pp. 389–90.

5. Be Peacemakers

1. Siman 46:4: A person must say the Blessings *shelo asani goy* (Who did not make me a non-Jew), *shelo asani aved* (Who did not make me a slave) and *shelo asani isha* (Who did not make me a woman) every day.

2. J. R. W. Stott, *God's New Society: The message of Ephesians*, The Bible Speaks Today, Downers Grove, IL: InterVarsity Press, 1979.

3. Stott, *God's New Society*.

4. Ephesians 2:11–18.

5. For a challenging exploration of what this means for the nature of our churches, see A. E. Walls, "The Ephesian Moment", in A. E. Walls, *The Cross-Cultural Process in Christian History*, T. & T. Clark, 2002, pp. 72–81.

6. Ephesians 4:3.

7. Matthew 5:9.

8. For the urgency of breaking down generational differences in church life, see K. Powell and C. Clark, *Sticky Faith: Everyday Ideas to Build Lasting Faith in Your Kids*, Zondervan, 2011, or J. Clark, *Mend the Gap*, IVP, 2007.

6. Be Unshakeable

1. 1,523 out of 2,228 passengers and crew were drowned during the sinking of the *Titanic* – a loss of 68 per cent. But according to Peter Brierley's research, out of every ten children aged 0–9 in Sunday school in 1985, only three were still connected with the church in 2005. See P. Brierley, "Have 'Youth Workers' Worked?", in P. Brierley, *UK Church Statistics 2005–2011*, ADBC, 2011, p. 14.

2. Hebrews 12:1–3.

3. J. Gliek, *FSTR: The acceleration of just about everything*, Vintage, 2000.

4. *Daft Punk*, October 2001.

5. See L. T. Johnson, *Hebrews: A Commentary*, John Knox Press, 2006, p. 57.

6. Indeed, the writer to the Hebrews describes our future as an "unshakable kingdom" (Hebrews 12:26–29).

7. Be Available

1. The commentator Marshall McLuhan argued that technology is always an attempt to extend the senses. See the now famous interview in *Playboy Magazine*, March 1969.

2. Nicholas Carr argues that our brains are actually being rewired through the process of being online, shortening our attention spans. N. Carr, *The Shallows – what the internet is doing to our brains*, Atlantic Press, 2010.

3. Matthew 1:20–23.

4. Matthew 28:20.

5. Information technology guru Clay Shirky makes a strong case for the ways in which social media present us with new opportunities for community and collaborating to make a difference in the world. C. Shirky, *Here Comes Everybody: The power of organizing without organisations*, Allen Lane, 2008.

6. For more ideas see T. Chester and S. Timmis, *Everyday Church: Mission by being good neighbours*, IVP, 2011.

8. Be Descendants

1. Philippians 2:3–11.

2. G. F. Hawthorne, *Philippians*, Word Biblical Commentary, Vol. 43, Word, 2004, p. 104.

3. J. Hutton, *A History of the Moravian Church* (2nd ed., 1909), Grand Rapids, Christian Classics Ethereal Library, www.ccel.org/ccel/hutton/moravian.v.vi.html

4. For a powerful, moving and profound Christian response to the Haiti disaster, see K. Annan, *Aftershock: Searching for honest faith when your world is shaken*, IVP, 2011.

Annan adds a 1 to the estimated death toll to "hang on to the personal scale of loss".

9. Be Go-betweens

1. We are a foster family, so exact numbers of children in our house are always difficult to predict.

2. Hebrews 4:14–16.

3. O'Brien argues that a key factor was that the recipients of this letter "were tired of bearing the shame of living outside their cultural heritage". P. T. O'Brien, *The Letter to the Hebrews*, The Pillar New Testament Commentary, Eerdmans, 2010, p. 13.

4. W. Lane, "Hebrews", in R. P. Martin and P. H. Davids, *Dictionary of the Later New Testament and its Developments* (electronic ed.), InterVarsity Press, 2000.

5. The threefold office of Jesus as Prophet, Priest and King can be a helpful way to understand his ministry in the world.

6. Leviticus 4:3.

7. 1 Peter 2:9.

10. Be Luminous

1. John 9:1–5.

2. For a powerful treatment of the problem of suffering, read C. S. Lewis, *The Problem of Pain*, HarperCollins, 2001.

3. Rick Warren put this well in the first sentence of a best-selling book: "It's not about you." R. Warren, *The Purpose Driven Life*, Zondervan, 2002, p. 17.

4. Matthew 5:14–16.

5. Matthew 5:14–16.

11. Say It Audibly

1. The closest I have come across is Chapter XVII of Francis' *Rule* of 1221, when he instructed the friars not to preach unless they had the necessary permission to do so. Then he added, "Let all the brothers, however, preach by their deeds." www.americancatholic.org/Messenger/Oct2001/Wiseman.asp

2. Mark 1:15.

3. Acts 10:36–38.

4. Acts 10:39–43.

5. Observation made by David Westlake, Evangelical Alliance Council, 2010.

6. 1 Peter 3:1ff.

7. 1 Peter 1:23.

8. E. P. Clowney, *The Message of 1 Peter: The way of the cross*, The Bible Speaks Today, IVP, 1988, p. 130.

9. M. Green, *Evangelism in the Early Church*, Highland Books, 1990, p. 42.

12. Say It Empathetically

1. 1 Peter 2:21.
2. John 14:1–4.
3. John 19:26–27.
4. Luke 23:39–43.

13. Say It Honestly

1. R. Gutman, "The Hidden Power of Smiling", TED talk, 2011, www.ted.com/talks/ron_gutman_the_hidden_power_of_smiling.html
2. Matthew 26:36–39.
3. For an exploration of what this kind of lack of emotional engagement does to Christian leadership, see S. Walker, *The Undefended Leader Trilogy*, Piquant, 2007.
4. For an exploration of emotions in the Christian life, see R. Edwards, *Religious Affections*, Banner of Truth, 1961.
5. J. Edwards, *The Words of Jonathan Edwards in Two Volumes*, Vol. 1, Paternoster, 1834, p. 238.
6. See J. I. Packer, *A Passion for Holiness*, Crossway, 1992.
7. www.wordmadeflesh.org/the-cry/the-cry-vol-7-no-4/only-the-suffering-god-can-help/ These themes are picked up in J. Moltmann's famous work, *The Crucified God: The Cross of Christ as the Foundation and Criticism of Christian Theology*, Fortress, 1993.
8. See K. Kandiah, *Dyscipleship: Why I fall asleep when I pray and 12 other discipleship dysfunctions*, Authentic, 2009.

14. Say It Creatively

1. J. Didion, *The White Album*, cited in J. Krakauer, *Into Thin Air*, Pan, 1997, p. 123.
2. Acts 3:15.
3. Mark 4:30–34.
4. N. T. Wright, "How can the Bible be authoritative?", *Vox Evangelica*, 1991, 21:22.
5. See Luke 8:9–10.
6. For more on the idea of using Jesus' stories in evangelism, see P. Weston, "Evangelicals and Evangelism", in I. Taylor, *Not Evangelical Enough! – The gospel at the centre*, Carlisle: Paternoster, 2003, pp. 137–52.

15. Say It Compassionately

1. John 8:4–11.
2. John 9:39.
3. D. Kinnaman, *Unchristian: What a New Generation Really Thinks about Christianity… and Why It Matters*, Baker, 2007.
4. M. L. King, "A time to break the silence", sermon at Riverside Church, New York, 4 April 1967, cited in S. Claiborne, *The Irresistible Revolution*, Zonvervan, 2006, p. 153.

16. Say It Hopefully

1. Proverbs 18:21.

2. Proverbs 16:24.

3. Luke 23:38–43.

4. For a fuller exploration of this passage see K. Kandiah and M. Kandiah, *How to Save a Life*, Authentic, 2009.

5. Etymologically, "excruciating" comes from the Latin *excruciatus*: *ex-* = "out of, from" and *cruciare* = "to crucify".

6. Hot drinks are prohibited by the Church of the Latter Day Saints (Mormons).

7. My understanding of God's work in the life of a Mormon is that God is keen to draw all people to true knowledge of Jesus. God will use all sorts of circumstances and opportunities to do that, as Paul points out to a group of pagan philosophers in Athens: "From one man he made all the nations, that they should inhabit the whole earth; and he marked out their appointed times in history and the boundaries of their lands. God did this so that they would seek him and perhaps reach out for him and find him, though he is not far from any one of us" (Acts 17:26–27). These points of contact make a bridge in people's lives for them to hear the gospel. For more on this idea, see A. McGrath, *Bridge Building: Effective Christian Apologetics*, IVP, 1992.

17. Say It Absolutely

1. Luke 6:37.

2. Matthew 6:12.

3. Luke 23:26–34.

4. John 1:29.

5. Psalm 103:12.

6. Matthew 6; Luke 6:37–38; Matthew 18:21–35.

7. Luke 6:37.

8. Thomas Merton, cited in J. C. Arnold, *Seventy Times Seven*, Plough, 1998, p. 145.

9. The full prayer can be accessed here: www.orthodoxytoday.org/articles/VelimirovichBlessEnemies.php

18. Say It Critically

1. K. Fox, *Watching the English: The Hidden Rules of English Behaviour*, Hodder & Stoughton, 2005, pp. 138ff.

2. Revelation 5:5.

3. Luke 11:42–48, 52.

4. Ephesians 4:15.

5. 1 Peter 2:23.

6. For a great example of Jesus' challenge of religious and political power, see S. Claiborne, *Jesus for President*, Zondervan, 2008, p. 119.

7. Interestingly, one place where Christians try to emulate Jesus' harsh criticism is in response to "secular government". Strangely, our public engagement often lacks the love and compassion that Jesus demonstrated. For a fascinating discussion of this topic, see O. Guinness, *The Case for Civility*, HarperOne, 2008. He says about the American context: "The religious right has become the best argument for its worst opponents, the most powerful factor in its own rejection, and a prime reason for the repudiation of religion in contemporary America", p. 103.

8. W. Berry, *Citizenship Papers*, Shoemaker and Hoard, 2003, p. 14, cited in Guinness, *The Case for Civility*, p. 93.

19. Say It Confidently

1. Os Guinness comments on the victim language being used increasingly by Western Christians: "those who portray themselves as victims come to perceive themselves as victims and then to paralyse themselves as victims…" O. Guinness, *The Case for Civility*, HarperOne, 2008, p. 93.

2. John 19:6–12.

3. John 19:8.

4. Acts 4:13.

5. 2 Timothy 1:7.

6. Questions around belief in a sovereign God and the problem of suffering often lead to discussion of human freedom. For an excellent treatment of these issues, see D. A. Carson, *How Long, O Lord?: Reflections on Suffering and Evil*, IVP, 2006, or J. I. Packer, *Evangelism and the Sovereignty of God*, IVP, 2010.

7. See Daniel 3 for an example of righteous resistance that led to more suffering but eventual salvation.

8. Luke 12:11–12.

20. Say It Silently

1. See J. Smith, *The Good and Beautiful God*, Hodder, 2011.

2. Luke 23:8–12.

3. Isaiah 53:7.

4. Matthew 7:6.

5. Similar instructions are given to us in Proverbs with the same sort of nuance: "Do not answer fools according to their folly, or you yourself will be just like them. Answer fools according to their folly, or they will be wise in their own eyes" (Proverbs 26:4–5).

6. W. C. Kaiser, Jr., P. H. Davids, F. F. Bruce and M. T. Brauch, *Hard Sayings of the Bible*, IVP, 1996, pp. 370–71.

7. You can see a similar logic at work in the shocking parable of the Rich Man and Lazarus in Luke 16:19–31.

21. Do Small

1. There are some great tips on living lightly in R. Valerio, *L is for Lifestyle: Christian Living That Doesn't Cost the Earth*, IVP, 2008.
2. Matthew 19:13–15.
3. Matthew 18:4.
4. Matthew 6:5–6.
5. Matthew 6:2–4.
6. Mark 12:42.
7. Matthew 8:20.

22. Do Work

1. "How Europeans Spend their Time, everyday life of women and men", *Euro Stat*, 2004.
2. See the study by Mark Aguair and Erik Hurst, www.stlouisfed.org/publications/re/articles/?id=43
3. This is an adaptation of a paraphrase, "The job of the newspaper is to comfort the afflicted and afflict the comfortable", from F. P. Dunne, *Newspaper Publicity*, R. H. Russell, 1902, p. 240.
4. John 4:31–38.
5. In fact, a large chunk of Jesus' ministry takes place around meals. See C. Gempf, *Mealtime Habits of the Messiah: 40 Encounters with Jesus*, Zondervan, 2005.
6. There are some excellent resources to help you further explore the relationship between work and worship, including: M. Greene, *Thank God It's Monday*, Scripture Union, 2001; R. P. Stevens and A. Ung, *Taking Your Soul to Work: Overcoming the Nine Deadly Sins of the Workplace*, Eerdmans, 2010.
7. O. Guinness, *The Call: Finding and Fulfilling the Central Purpose of Your Life*, Thomas Nelson, 2003, p. 29.
8. See K. Kandiah, *Twenty-Four: Integrating faith and everyday life*, Authentic, 2007.
9. One of the biggest frustrations many people face in the current economic climate is not being able to find paid employment at all. When we talk about vocation and work here, we are not talking exclusively about paid employment, although people often conflate the two.

23. Do Nothing

1. Apologies to my vegetarian readers!
2. See J. R. Edwards, *The Gospel According to Mark*, The Pillar New Testament Commentary, Apollos, 2002, p. 11.
3. Mark 6:31–34.
4. Matthew 11:28–30.
5. M. Green, *The Message of Matthew: The kingdom of heaven*, The Bible Speaks Today, IVP, 2000, p. 143.
6. Matthew 11:28–29 The Message.

24. Do Something

1. Matthew 9:35–38.

2. L. Newbigin, *The Light Has Come*, Eerdmans, 1982, p. 63.

3. For a further exploration of these themes, see T. Keller, *Ministries of Mercy: The Call of the Jericho Road*, P & R Publishing, 1997.

4. "Integral mission or holistic transformation is the proclamation and demonstration of the gospel. It is not simply that evangelism and social involvement are to be done alongside each other. Rather, in integral mission our proclamation has social consequences as we call people to love and repentance in all areas of life and our social involvement has evangelistic consequences as we bear witness to the transforming grace of Jesus Christ." From the Micah Declaration, cited in T. Chester (ed.), *Justice, Mercy and Humility: Integral mission and the poor*, Authentic, 2002, p. 2.

5. See L. Newbigin, *Sign of the Kingdom*, Eerdmans, 1980, for more on this theme of the mission of the church as a foretaste of the coming Kingdom.

6. Revelation 21:4.

7. Matthew 25:41–45.

8. T. Keller, *Generous Justice: How God's Grace Makes Us Just*, Hodder, 2010, p. 188.

25. Do Viral

1. As of November 2011.

2. C. Shirky, *Here Comes Everybody: The power of organizing without organizations*, Allen Lane, 2008.

3. Open Doors maintains a watch-list of the countries where Christians are most at risk of persecution or oppression. Countries such as North Korea, Iran, Afghanistan, Saudi Arabia and Pakistan feature heavily on this list. www.opendoors.uk.org

4. D. Bonhoeffer, *The Cost of Discipleship*, SCM, 1959, p. 79 (page reference from 1996 edition).

5. R. Allen, *The Spontaneous Expansion of the Church*, Wipf and Stock, 1997.

6. Matthew 4:18–22.

7. "It was something new that Jesus took the initiative and called those whom he would have as disciples." L. Morris, *The Gospel According to Matthew*, The Pillar New Testament Commentary, IVP, 1992, p. 84.

8. Matthew 28:18–20.

9. D. Willard, *The Great Omission: Reclaiming Jesus' essential teachings on discipleship*, HarperOne, 2006.

10. See W. A. Henrichsen, *Disciples are Made not Born*, Victor Books, 1988.

11. L. Newbigin, *The Household of God: Lectures on the Nature of the Church*, SCM Press, 1953, p. ix.

26. Do Sabbath

1. John 5:16–18.

2. It almost goes without saying that, inspired by the resurrection of Jesus which took place on the first day of the week, Christians started to gather on Sundays rather than the Sabbath day (Friday evening to Saturday afternoon). There is one reference that alludes to this idea in Revelation 1:10, where the "Lord's day" is mentioned. "The Lord's day, while fulfilling all the beneficent purposes of God in the institution of the Sabbath for mankind, was kept 'not under the old written code but in the new life of the Spirit' (Rom. 7:6)." A. S. Wood, "Lord's Day", in D. R. W. Wood, I. H. Marshall, A. R. Millard, J. I. Packer and D. J. Wiseman (eds), *New Bible Dictionary* (3rd ed.), IVP, 1996, p. 694.

3. See Deuteronomy 5:12–15, which is a retelling of the Ten Commandments with a different emphasis.

4. Mark 3:1–6.

5. Luke 13:10–17.

6. John 5:16.

7. Mark 1:30.

8. John 9:14.

9. Mark 1:25.

10. Mark 2:23–28.

11. Hebrews 4:9.

27. Do Miracles

1. John 20:30.

2. Cessationists believe that some of, if not all of the spiritual gifts are not in operation today. See M. J. Houghton, "A Re-examination of 1 Corinthians 13:8–13", *Bibliotheca Sacra*, Vol. 153 (611), Dallas Theological Seminary, 1996, p. 343.

3. Houghton, "A Re-examination of 1 Corinthians 13:8–13", p. 353.

4. John 14:12.

5. B. Johnson, *The Supernatural Power of a Transformed Mind: Access to a Life of Miracles*, Destiny Image, 2009, p. 63, argued that a legal problem persisted in their church for a long time because they had not prayed in the correct way: "I had been binding what wasn't free to function in heaven, but I wasn't replacing it with anything… I have been binding the spirit of injustice, but we need to loose the spirit of justice." This seems to be an example of what Pete Greig argues against in his excellent book, *God on Mute: Engaging the silence of unanswered prayer*, Kingsway, 2007, p. 43: "I was also scared that Sammy might die if I didn't pray enough, or if I didn't have enough faith, or if I didn't fast enough, or if I didn't bind some disembodied principality…"

6. John 6:25–33.

7. For a very powerful illustration of this, see the parable that Jesus teaches in Luke 16:19–31.

8. 1 Corinthians 13:8–13.

9. Psalm 22 is a classic case, and it is underlined by the fact that it is the psalm Jesus quotes from the agony of the cross.

10. Daniel 3:16–18.

11. Habakkuk 3:17–19.

28. Do Revolution

1. Mark 11:12–17.

2. John 2:14–15.

3. Hosea 9:10–11: "When I found Israel, it was like finding grapes in the desert; when I saw your ancestors, it was like seeing the early fruit on the fig tree." See also L. Ryken, J. Wilhoit, T. Longman, C. Duriez, D. Penney and D. G. Reid, *Dictionary of Biblical Imagery*, IVP, 2000, p. 283.

4. Mark 9:42.

5. J. R. Edwards, *The Gospel According to Mark*, The Pillar New Testament, IVP, 2002, p. 343.

29. Do Touch

1. Luke 7:11–16.

2. J. Nolland, *Luke 1:1 – 9:20*, Word Biblical Commentary, Vol. 35A, Word, 2002, p. 323.

3. John 11:38ff.

4. Numbers 19:16.

5. S. Hipps, *Flickering Pixels: How technology shapes your faith*, Zondervan, 2009, p. 108.

6. A concept that is applied to doctors and health professionals who have worked closely with suffering people. See P. Huggard, "Compassion Fatigue: How much can I give?" in S. Barrett, C. Komaromy, M. Robb and A. Rogers, *Communication, Relationships and Care: A Reader*, Routledge, 2003, p. 194.

30. Do Together

1. Luke 10:17–23.

2. C. G. Cruse, "Apostle" in J. B. Green, S. McKnight and I. H. Marshall, *Dictionary of Jesus and the Gospels*, IVP, 1992, p. 31.

3. Some translations count 70 disciples and 70 nations, others 72 disciples and 72 nations.

4. Luke 10:8–12.

5. See the chapter "The Logic of Election" in L. Newbigin, *The Gospel in a Pluralist Society*, SPCK, 1989, pp. 80ff.

6. Luke 10:3.

7. John 16:1–4.

8. Revelation 21:27.